Children's Ministry That Fits

Beyond One-Size-Fits-All Approaches
to Nurturing Children's Spirituality

David M. Csinos

Foreword by Joyce E. Bellous
Afterword by Brian D. McLaren

GW00566863

WIPF & STOCK · Eugene, Oregon

CHILDREN'S MINISTRY THAT FITS
Beyond One-Size-Fits-All Approaches to Nurturing Children's Spirituality

Wipf & Stock
An Imprint of Wipf and Stock Publishers
199 W. 8th Ave., Suite 3
Eugene, OR 97401

www. wipfandstock.com

ISBN 13: 978-1-61097-121-8

Manufactured in the U.S.A.

Children's Ministry That Fits

In memory of
JAMES WILLIAM MACLELLAN
with whom I shared my childhood.

Contents

Foreword

Dave Csinos's book is situated within an important conversation that we're not yet having in North American churches. It's a conversation that asks questions about children's experience in ways that draw us into educational involvement with them on Sunday mornings as well as through the week. Questions such as: What currently moves children to think, feel, wonder and act? What do they want to discuss? What do they believe about how the world began and how it will end? What matters to them? What do they hope for? How do they feel and think about the future? What do the symbols of the church mean to them? How do they aspire to make the world a better place? What do they want to do for God and for the world? Education has these questions at its heart if it's actually working to enable the young to grow up into the Christian faith. That conversation is the purpose of Christian education.

This book takes Christian education seriously. There are layers beneath its research and inquiry, some of which echo my own story. In 1993, I came kicking and screaming to my post in Christian education at a Canadian seminary. I was trained as an analytical philosopher who moved into continental philosophy at the PhD level by analyzing Michel Foucault's description of power, to understand the nature of social relations. What was I doing teaching Christian education in a North American seminary where, for the most part, education is downplayed and downgraded? Worse than that, in the first few years, the primary question I got from students and churches, which I could never answer, was: What curriculum should I choose for our educational program?

How would I know? I wanted to shout. I don't know your people. I don't know your context. I don't know your congregation's gifts. I don't know what you've been trying to do. I don't know what you aspire to accomplish through your overall educational goals. How could I possibly know what curriculum you should choose?

Yet I knew Christian educators must have two things: the Bible and a repertoire of embodied educational methods that draw learners into relationship with the living God. But it's hard to get that message across to people who struggle to capture a few guilt-ridden souls who can be pressed into teaching Sunday school—sometimes—but certainly not every week. In that early period of frustration, I wondered what people who say they are Christian actually believed about what it means to grow up into the fullness of God.

I still wonder about that. How can we inspire North Americans to care about their faith in God as a priority? How can this generation be moved to love God more than any other love?

In response to my position in Christian education, because of the way I was educated, I developed an approach that focused on Scripture as the holistic story of God's redemptive involvement in our lives and as an invitation to become God's friends. I taught Socrates' conversation, Aristotle's deliberation, Kant's conceptual analysis, Rousseau's empowering, experiential learning, Hegel's experiencing, Freire's problem-posing learning, as well as other twentieth-century teaching methods. You can imagine how I alarmed those students who still wanted me to tell them what curriculum they should choose for their educational programs.

What surprised me, as I worked out how to teach Christian education, was the biblical openness to these teaching methods. Jesus used conversation, reason and experiential learning, to name a few of his many educational practices. Methods I wanted students to learn had been used throughout the history of Christianity. Who knew?

Then came another blow. God called me to focus on children's spirituality. Unfair, I complained. Isn't it bad enough that you drew me into Christian education after I climbed the academic ladder to educational philosophy? Now you want me to stoop to children's ministry. What a full member of our unhappy, child-devaluing culture I truly was at that point. I'm indebted to British colleagues for putting up with my arrogance and waiting for me to catch up with their passion for teaching the young.

Like Dave, I'm persuaded that the North American church's greatest need is for intelligent, imaginative, passionate, action-oriented life-long learning. It's time for believers to expect and understand that being Christian calls us to learn our way of life—in terms of daily practice within a broad understanding of Christianity. It was through involvement in children's spirituality that I came to see the need for, and got a glimpse of, the broad picture into which biblically sound educational practice finds its most inclusive role, a picture that developed through spirituality research.

Spiritual styles research, formed and carried out in collaboration with Dave and others, was undertaken during engagement with an international group of religious educators who are motivated by their love for working with children. As part of that research, Dave discovered that children relate to God, church culture and religious experiences by using words, emotion, symbols, and action. The four styles he explores and explains in this book are embedded in Christian history and are inclusive of children from many denominations, traditions, and contexts. But why do spiritual styles matter?

The issue is that Christian denominations tend toward a dominant approach to spirituality that focuses on one or perhaps two of these styles, to the exclusion of the others. There's a way to be Anglican and a way to be Pentecostal—and these cultures are usually very different from one another. But children born into or brought to these cultures are diverse in the way they express their spiritual lives. If church settings fail to be inclusive of all four spiritual styles, children feel left out. If they feel excluded, they may think there's something wrong with them. Eventually, they may come to believe there's something wrong with God. When we develop educational settings for the young that include what really matters to them, they're more likely to believe that the Christian church is a welcoming, important place.

It's my conviction that intelligent, passionate, compassionate faith is hard to learn. Unless we get serious, our educational church programs won't captivate the imagination of this generation. If we fail to draw children into knowing God, and Jesus Christ, whom God sent, their capacity to comprehend and resist the unique cocktail of worldliness that constitutes the present moment is underdeveloped and weak. It will not save them from slavery to the world.

When I reflect on the conditions of this current age, I recall that we're called to be people of hope. Over the years, I witnessed the growth of a younger generation of Christian leaders who care about ministry. Dave is one of these younger leaders and his book is a significant part of an informed, mature, reasoned, intentional, wise response to the spiritual needs of children. Thanks be to God!

Please read this book attentively. In it, you'll find theoretically sound, useful approaches to teaching and nurturing children so that your educational culture and ministerial context can be a place of inclusion, respect and spiritual conversation that will inform and inspire you, just as much as it welcomes and challenges children to want to be God's friends.

Joyce E. Bellous
author of *Educating Faith*,
Conversations That Change Us, and *For Crying Out Loud*

Acknowledgments

WRITING A BOOK IS never a solitary endeavor. As I engaged in the research, writing, and publication of this book, several people have offered me their time, insight, and encouragement.

First, I'd like to take a moment to express my gratitude for Jim Tedrick, Christian Amondson, and the wonderful people at Wipf and Stock who guided me through the publishing process. Thank you for your willingness to take a chance on this fresh, young author. I am also grateful for my editor, Kathleen DuVall, whose careful eye made sure the book said what I hoped it would say.

Pioneer Clubs graciously supported me in my research through the Virginia C. Patterson Continuing Education Scholarship. Their financial support helped equip me to carry out my research to the best of my abilities. I am grateful for Judy Bryson, who saw my potential at the Children's Spirituality Conference and encouraged me to apply for financial assistance.

I would like to acknowledge the guidance and support that I received from many friends and colleagues in this project. The infamous Wheaton class, under the leadership of Don Ratcliff, Scottie May, and Chris Boyatzis, journeyed with me through the process of developing the research on which this book is based. I am forever indebted to this community of co-learners who shared with one another many of the ideas that I utilized during my research and writing. Your friendship and assistance from this book's conception to consummation is greatly appreciated.

I'm grateful for Karen Szala-Meneok, who was incredibly helpful in having my research receive approval from the McMaster Research Ethics Board, for Caitlin Scherer, who served as my research assistant during the focus group meetings, and for James Peterson and Phil Zylla, who offered wise comments on early drafts of this book.

I'd like to acknowledge the indispensable role of the people who were directly involved in my fieldwork. Without the assistance of the pastors, staff members, and parents from Townsend Baptist Church, Northview Community Church, and Lawrence Park Presbyterian Church, this book wouldn't have gotten off the ground. I am incredibly thankful for the thirteen children who took the time to talk with me about their lives, and their families, for their parents' willingness to drive the children to and from meetings, put up with my incessant emails and phone calls, and meet with me to chat about their children. You are the heart and soul of this book.

I would be remiss if I didn't pause to express my appreciation for two of my closest mentors. From the first time we met, Joyce Bellous guided me not only through my research but also through some important decisions and transitions in life. Her constant willingness to offer advice, encouragement, and criticism as I researched and wrote was greatly appreciated. For the past few years, Brian McLaren has been a key source of inspiration, motivation, and guidance in my work, ministry, and day-to-day life. His gentle soul, compassionate faith, and humble spirit continue to offer me glimpses of a new kind of Christianity and remind me what real ministry looks like. I am honored to have the words of these gracious individuals open and close this book. It has been a privilege to have you as mentors, colleagues, and friends.

Finally, I would like to express my thanks to my family. My in-laws have been helpful in several ways during the writing of this book, but I'm especially grateful to them for providing my wife and me with many, many delicious meals and opening their home as a "place to flop."

Since beginning this book nearly five years ago, my parents and sister have been extraordinarily encouraging and caring to me in my studies and writing. They have seen me through the highs and lows and have always been there to push me forward. And the addition of my brother-in-law to the family a few years ago has only increased the mutual joy and support in our family. Mom, Dad, Ann and Michael: thank you for giving me wings to fly and for always being a soft place to land.

As life has become increasingly hectic and unpredictable, my wife, Jenny, has been my solid rock, keeping me grounded and providing me with a model of love, tenderness, humility, and compassion for all people. Words, emotion, symbols, and action cannot convey my affection, admiration, and appreciation for you. Westley said it best: "This is true love—you think this happens every day?"[1]

---

1. *The Princess Bride*, directed by Rob Reiner, Twentieth Century Fox, 1987.

Do I Have to Go to the Basement?

IN THE LATE SPRING of 2006, I took a trip to Chicago that would turn into a profound, life-changing spiritual journey into the realm of childhood, spirituality, and ministry. Towards the end of May, I climbed aboard the train in my home city in southern Ontario and began a ten-hour ride to the Windy City. The purpose of this trip was to be involved in a graduate course on researching children's spirituality and ministry models at Wheaton College, held in conjunction with the 2006 Children's Spirituality Conference: Christian Perspectives.

Many of us who were involved in this course had descended on Chicago from across the continent (one co-learner had even flown in from Hong Kong), so most of us were meeting one another for the first time when we walked into our classroom in the Billy Graham Center and crossed the threshold into what would be a defining week in many of our lives. In order to remedy this unfamiliarity, our esteemed guides on this journey—Don Ratcliff, Scottie May, and Chris Boyatzis—asked us to share two of our most vivid and meaningful childhood spiritual experiences: one positive and one negative.

After some reflection, I shared with the group the particularly negative experience I had during the one and only time that I participated in my church's children's liturgy program. I remember bawling in the corner of the room because I just wanted to be back upstairs in the sanctuary. Before that day, my parents had encouraged me to attend children's liturgy, but they never pressured me to go if I didn't want to. After that fateful day when I descended the steps and showed my face at children's liturgy, I don't remember my parents asking me if I wanted to go to the basement again—at least not until I was a teenager, when they would offer to walk down with me as a joke.

Growing up in the Roman Catholic Church, I attended church with my family at Holy Redeemer, a parish led by the Redemptorist priests. Although children's liturgy was a weekly ministry at our church, I never felt compelled to participate in it. I preferred to remain in the sanctuary with my mother, father, and sister for the entirety of the Mass.

Looking back, I now realize that there were two significant reasons that I wanted to stay upstairs with my family. First, I appreciated experiencing the Mass with my parents and sister, my spiritual guides. Since they were the primary influences on my spiritual life, I didn't understand why I should leave them for the greater part of the Mass. Second, I had come to value the richness, reverence, and holiness embodied in the rituals and symbols that I encountered at Holy Redeemer. Attending children's liturgy would mean that I had to remove myself from the spiritually-saturated sanctuary, with its liturgical colors, symbols, and rites, and go to the drab, dull, and boring basement. There may have been cookies and crafts down there, but these sweet treats and creative activities could not compete with the transcendental traditions of the Mass and the symbolic beauty of the church building.

After sharing this story with the class at Wheaton, I began to wonder if I was alone in this childhood experience. Perhaps there are many children, I thought, who attend children's liturgy, Sunday school, or other age-segregated ministries, but would rather stay with their families or remain in the sanctuary for "grown-up" services. I wondered if the people, places, and objects in congregations affected other children as powerfully as they had affected me. I made the most of my co-learners and guides at Wheaton and began forming a research project that would allow me to explore how places, objects, and people in churches affect children's experiences with God. And more than a year later, with the kind and skillful assistance of Joyce Bellous, this research study came into fruition. This book draws heavily from that project, which I undertook from September 2007 to February 2008. It is the direct result of the journey to Chicago that would leave an imprint on my heart and mind for years to come.

Through my conversations with children during these six months, I started to observe four distinct yet fluid ways that young people encounter God, participate in their congregations, and make meaning of the world around them. These ways of knowing God are *spiritual styles,*[1] four legitimate, powerful ways through which human beings transcend the here and now, connect with God, and understand our surroundings. Spiritual styles have the power to affect us at our very core and they act as lenses through which we see and make sense of the world around us. Spiritual styles touch the very heart of our innermost being—and they are certainly at the heart of this book. As you move from page to page, chapter to chapter, I'd like to take you on a journey to explore four ways of knowing God that, when taken together, are harmoniously dissonant.[2]

If you are reading this book, I imagine that you have a love for children and a desire to help them experience God in profound and life-changing ways. You probably fall into at least one of the following three categories.

Perhaps you're someone who works with children in a congregation, school, organization, or some other ministry setting. Whether you are a children's pastor, a Christian educator, a Sunday school teacher, or a lay leader, this book will help you to explore the spiritual needs of children and discover how you can nurture the faith and spirituality of young people in an environment of inclusive hospitality. I would encourage you to use the material I present in these pages to critically reflect on your ministries in order to ensure that all the children in your midst are being welcomed, nurtured, and included.

Maybe you're a parent who yearns for your children to experience spiritual growth and formation. You may be seeking advice on how to raise spiritually-healthy children who have personal encounters with the living God. Even though this book is primarily intended for practitioners, parents can gain much insight from it and should have little difficulty transferring the ideas for congregations into homes and families. It is my hope that this book can assist you in understanding the spiritual styles that affect your children and in gaining practical, thoughtful information about how to cultivate their spiritual lives.

Finally, you may be a seminary student or professional researcher who seeks insight into the spiritual lives of children. I encourage you to

1. Bellous et al., *Spiritual Styles.* Bellous et al., *Spiritual Styles—Children's Version.*

2. Some of the material in this book has been previously published in the *International Journal of Children's Spirituality, Lifelong Faith,* and the *Journal of Childhood and Religion.*

open yourself to the concept of spiritual styles, the methods of research that I used in the study that led to this book, and the material that I present regarding strategies and tactics for nurturing children. The implications of spiritual styles in the lives of children are immeasurable and further research is needed if we are to fully understand how spiritual styles affect children's experiences with God and their faith communities. I invite you to join me in this journey and begin exploring spiritual styles for yourself.

Whether you are a pastor, parent, student, or scholar (or someone else altogether), I commend you for your desire to learn how to better minister to children. Thank you for joining me on this journey alongside children. May our loving God guide you as you seek to nurture (and, in turn, be nurtured by) the children that the Lord has graciously brought into your midst.

As I have already mentioned, my reflections on my childhood experiences led me to wonder about how people and places at congregations affect the spiritual lives of children. The questions I began asking propelled me into the world of children's spirituality and meaning making. In the first chapter of this book, I outline the assumptions and theories regarding childhood, spirituality, and meaning making that form the bedrock for the material that I present in subsequent chapters. We'll walk together through a number of paradigms for children and take a jaunt through the realm of object relations theory in order to better understand the young companions that we are seeking to nurture.

In the second chapter, I introduce you to some friends that I came to know during my research in 2007 and 2008. They are the research participants—thirteen children from three different congregations—and their lives form the backbone of this book. After telling you a little bit about them and their faith communities, I move on to explain the methods that I used in my research, the ways in which I engaged these young people in conversation about their spiritual lives. Whether in a ministry, home, or research setting, it is vital for adults to develop skills that help them to accurately hear the voices of children. The methods I explore in this chapter can be useful for adults in discovering the dominant spiritual styles of the children in their lives and listening to their voices with accuracy, responsibility, and respect.

After talking with these thirteen children for several months, I began to notice that each of them demonstrated a dominant style of spirituality that seemed to affect how they experienced God and made meaning of the people and places in their lives. In chapter 3, I present an overview of these four spiritual styles—word, emotion, symbol, and action—and I describe how they are manifested in the lives of these thirteen children.

The fourth chapter builds on my discussion of spiritual styles by describing how children make use of the styles in their experiences with God, their interactions with their faith communities, and their day-to-day living. We gain an understanding of the spiritual lives of my thirteen young friends by exploring their words, actions, interests, and joys. Who helps them to experience God? How do they feel about their congregations? What do they do to nurture their relationships with God? These are just some of the questions that I address in chapter 4.

In the next three chapters, I present practical advice for those seeking to welcome and nurture the spiritual lives of all children. The ideas I offer can help pastors, teachers, and parents to meet the spiritual needs of young disciples by creating environments in which all children are included, embraced, and nurtured. Drawing from theory, practice, and personal experiences, I put forward two broad strategies that nurture children from all spiritual styles. In chapter 5, I focus on welcoming and including children in faith communities. Chapter 6 is devoted to the story strategy, to nurturing children through telling personal stories, hearing God's story, and linking the two together in their lived experiences.

Chapter 7 moves from strategies to tactics, from broad, long-term approaches to particular methods and ideas that emerge on the frontlines of ministry. By relying on the ways in which my thirteen conversation partners were affected by their spiritual styles, I explore some tactics for ministry with children that have the power to form and transform the lives of young people. In this way, I help these children to have a voice in suggesting how faith communities can meet their spiritual needs. When employed, these tactics work together to create environments in which all children fit—environments that are harmoniously dissonant.

In chapter 8, I offer some concluding reflections to the journey that this book has taken us on. My words on these pages are by no means the final words on the topic of spiritual styles and children. They are meant to serve as a starting point, the beginning of what I hope will prove to be a fruitful quest.

Through conversation and personal reflection with my fellow learners at Wheaton College, I began a journey into the inner lives of young people. When I stepped off the Metra train at the College Avenue station and was warmly greeted by Scottie May, I brought great expectations and high hopes along with my luggage. I'd made the trek from Ontario to Illinois to immerse myself in ideas, theories, and practices surrounding the spiritual lives of children. But nothing could have prepared me for the way in which a few simple questions and some self-reflection would impregnate me with the embryonic beginnings of a quest that would eventually lead to a new way of understanding children, spirituality, and ministry.

My conversations with thirteen young friends granted me a window into the inner lives of children—what makes them tick, how they encounter the living God, the ways in which they perceive the world around them, and how adults can nurture their spiritual lives. As I undertook this journey into the inner lives of children, I have been amazed, mystified, and awestruck at the remarkable and astonishing lives of my thirteen young guides. As we talked with one another, I could not help feeling as though I was encountering the holy, much like Moses when he first approached that burning bush. As you reflect on the spiritual lives of these thirteen children and the young people that have special places in your heart, I pray that you may also sense that you are standing on holy ground. And so the journey begins.

1

Laying a Solid Foundation

Making Meaning of Childhood, Spirituality, and Christian Faith

EVERY WEEKEND, COUNTLESS CHILDREN attend Sunday morning pro-grams at local congregations. They meet in different types of spaces, including church basements, classrooms, gymnasiums, movie theatres, and private homes. They interact with many leaders—parents, profes-sional Christian educators, lay Sunday school teachers, and teenagers, to name a few. From the number of books, curricula, resources, and web-sites dedicated to the spiritual formation of young people, it is evident that children's ministry has emerged as a legitimate and integral branch of the life of the church, one that is specifically aimed at meeting the spiritual needs of congregations' youngest members. I'm encouraged to see that pastors, parents, and laypeople are taking notice of the vital task of nurturing the spirituality of children.

Yet despite this boom in resources, important questions about the spiritual life of children and ministry models utilized to meet their spiritual needs remain unanswered. Worse yet, sometimes these questions aren't even asked. The result of this silence means that the spiritual needs of children can easily be neglected or inappropriately addressed and ministries can miss the mark as they aim to nurture children's spiritual lives. This book helps to fill this silence by explor-ing what has come to be called *spiritual styles*—four ways of knowing God that affect children's spiritual experiences, ultimate concerns, and relationships with the world around them.

In this book, I explore how congregations can intentionally work to provide environments in which children of all spiritual styles can feel a sense of fit and inclusion. Through study, personal experience, and my walk with children along the spiritual journey, I examine the effectiveness of children's ministries and programs in order to create environments that welcome, include, and nurture all children. In particular, this book is heavily based on information that I gathered through research involving conversations and exercises with children from three congregations. While I'm aware that these faith communities and young people are not representative of every child and every church, religious tradition, and culture, they provide a solid working knowledge from which I can explore the spiritual lives of children.

Children are active spiritual meaning makers who can have authentic encounters with God in diverse ways. But amidst this diversity, four ways of connecting with God—four spiritual styles—appear to color children's spiritual experiences. Through words, emotion, symbols, and action, young people sense God's divine presence. Those who seek to nurture children's spiritual lives and foster authentic relationships with God ought to create environments that are inclusive and welcoming of children who express each and every spiritual style. These are harmoniously dissonant environments. Through this book, readers will come to understand what spiritual styles are, how children use them to connect with God, and how to create environments that are conducive to experiencing God within every spiritual style.

A SOLID FOUNDATION

A few months ago, after my wife and I moved back to Canada after living in the southeastern United States, we began watching home renovation shows on television. It's not unusual on some of these programs for homeowners to hire designers and contractors to build additions onto their houses. Sometimes, however, the addition of a new mudroom, a third bedroom, or a guest bathroom proves to be impossible because the foundation on which homeowners hoped to build isn't up to code. The concrete has not been reinforced and cannot withstand the weight of the rooms that were to be built on them. In these situations, homeowners and contractors are left to decide what to do—rip up the concrete and lay a solid, new foundation or come to terms with the fact that they just won't be able to build the rooms they hoped to add to their home.

This is an apt metaphor for the serious study of any subject. One must begin by laying a firm foundation on which the remainder of a book, essay, or project can be built. So, before jumping right into discussions about spiritual styles and offering advice for practitioners and parents, it's important for me to lay a solid foundation for the broad subject that we explore here: children's spirituality. To do so, I pose the following questions, to which I respond throughout this chapter: What is childhood? How is childhood related to spirituality and faith? What does Christian spirituality look like? How do young people make meaning of the world around them, including God and faith communities?

In the sections that follow, I respond to these questions by offering a theoretical and philosophical foundation for this book. For readers who may not be familiar with these issues and topics, this chapter introduces you to concepts that shape how people view and interact with children. For more experienced readers, the following pages allow you to come to know the ideas that ground the material in this book. Whether you're a children's minister, a scholar, an educator, a parent, or a grandparent, this chapter provides you with a brief overview of the ideas that form the foundation on which I build throughout the remaining seven chapters. Let us begin, then, by taking a closer look at the phenomenon of childhood, how it has been understood over the past few centuries, as well as what I understand it to be.

CHILDHOOD, HUMANITY, AND AGENCY

Almost half a century ago, historian Philippe Ariès concluded that childhood did not exist in the medieval world. He argued that until the medieval period gave way, children were typically seen as miniature adults.[1] By examining artwork created during and after the medieval period, it is possible to get a glimpse of this assertion.[2]

During the medieval years, painters often depicted children as small adults; their bodies represent the proportions one would expect

1. Ariès, *Centuries of Childhood*, 128.

2. Ariès, *Centuries of Childhood*, 33. Steven Mintz, in his exploration of childhood in the United States, has made similar arguments for artistic representations of children during the colonial and Romantic time periods. Mintz, *Huck's Raft*, 79. Likewise, Ariès argues that before the thirteenth century, children were often dressed like miniature adults. Ariès, *Centuries of Childhood*, 50. By window shopping at GapKids, Old Navy, Gymboree, Please Mum, and other children's clothing stores, one can see that dressing children in adult fashions has once again become common.

to see on fully-developed human beings. As the medieval period gave way to modernity, however, artists began to portray children with physical attributes that more accurately represented biological reality. Infants, for example, were painted with proportionately larger heads, chubbier cheeks, and shorter legs. Clearly, the transition from the medieval era to modernity marked a significant shift in the way the western world regarded children. Since this time there have been three broad paradigms or metaphors that have been used to describe the phenomenon of childhood.[3]

The Production Line

One view of children that emerged since the medieval years was that of raw material. Instruction, education, and curriculum were seen as the lines of mass production and adults were responsible for molding children into their predetermined designs.[4] This model reflects the philosophy of John Locke, the English philosopher who supposed that the mind of the child comes into the world as a blank piece of paper or, as it is more popularly termed, as a *tabula rasa*—a blank slate.[5] Several parallel conceptions to Locke's proposal continue to be widely held in the contemporary world, including metaphors for children as wet cement, which suggest that they are to be molded or written on by adults, or sponges, which passively soak up information presented by adults.

These paradigms for childhood form the backbone of what Paulo Freire refers to as the "banking" model of education. Rather than encouraging students to participate in the educational process through self-exploration and inquiry, the banking system turns education into "an act of depositing, in which the students are the depositories and the teacher is the depositor. Instead of communicating, the teacher . . . makes deposits which the students patiently receive, memorize, and repeat."[6]

This concept is not uncommon today, both within faith communities, through the Sunday school or church school, and outside of congregations, through systems of public education. Whether children are

---

3. This discussion is based on Westerhoff, *Will Our Children*, 100–101 and Westerhoff, "The Church's Contemporary Challenge."

4. Westerhoff, *Will Our Children*, 100. Westerhoff, "The Church's Contemporary Challenge," 356.

5. Locke, *Essay*, 104.

6. Freire, *Pedagogy of the Oppressed*, 72.

seen as raw material, blank slates, wet cement, or sponges, these metaphors espouse a view of young people as passive objects to be molded or formed into functioning human beings by adults.

The Greenhouse

With that advent of psychology and psychoanalysis, largely pioneered by Sigmund Freud, the production line model for childhood began to give way during the twentieth century. Theories of human development that started to emerge midway through the century, such as those put forward by Jean Piaget, Lawrence Kohlberg, and Erik Erikson, held that children needed to progress along a path of maturation. They were to gradually develop along a line from lower developmental stages to those that were higher and more complex.[7]

The greenhouse became the new paradigm for children, who were seen as divine seeds that needed to be nurtured in order to properly develop, mature, and grow. Adults, as the gardeners, were to ensure that the environments in which the children lived were appropriate for fostering healthy development. They had to make certain that "physical, spiritual, and educational setting[s] were well suited to growth."[8]

While both the production line and greenhouse analogies reflect common notions of their days (and even today), they both tend to rob children of agency. In the former model, children need adults to do things *to* them; in the latter, they need adults to do things *for* them.[9] Whether raw material or divine seeds, children are seen as largely (if not completely) dependent on adults for their formation, development, and growth—at least according to these metaphors. What's required, then, is a paradigm that values children as whole persons possessing agency and the ability to help themselves. We need a model in which adults do things *with* children.

The Pilgrim

Spearheaded by psychologist Robert Coles, such a paradigm emerged toward the end of the twentieth century: children as pilgrims. While conducting research with children, Coles made a discovery: "As the chil-

---

7. Westerhoff, *Will Our Children*, 100.

8. Sutherland, *Children in English-Canadian Society*, 18.

9. Westerhoff, "The Church's Contemporary Challenge," 356.

dren traveled the ordinary days of life, from time to time they sensed a spiritual purpose."[10] With this idea came a model in which children were seen as spiritual pilgrims, active agents who walk with adults on the journey of life rather than passively soaking up information according to the production line paradigm or banking model of education or simply passing through predetermined life stages according to the greenhouse metaphor.

This view of childhood radically alters how we do ministry with children and how we nurture their spiritual lives. It affirms their status as active makers of meaning, a quality of humanity that's at the heart of what it means to be a spiritual being.[11] Regarding children as pieces of raw material or as divine seeds fails to capture the natural and supernatural qualities of their spiritual lives.

This book finds its home in the paradigm of children as spiritual pilgrims, a model that values them as active agents who make meaning of themselves and the world around them. Rather than depriving them of agency by seeing them as blank slates, I hold that children are fellow spiritual pilgrims who take in, process, and make meaning of information in unique and personalized ways. Instead of presenting them with information that they are to passively take in and memorize, I propose that educators, parents, pastors, and other adults can best nurture the spiritual lives of children by walking with them on the journey. We can become co-learners with children in our quests to know God. At times, the adult leads the child forward along the path, and at other moments the child guides us as we seek together the presence of the living God.

THE SPIRITUAL LIVES OF CHILDREN

In the spring of 2007, I did what millions of others had done before me—I went online, entered my name and email address, created a password, and clicked "Sign Up." I created my Facebook profile. After adding some personal information and uploading a recent photo of myself (the most flattering one I could find, of course!), I began searching for friends.

During the next few weeks, I found Facebook friends around every cyber-corner. I was thrilled to be able to reconnect with former classmates and coworkers and I eagerly browsed through the details of their

10. Stonehouse, *Joining Children*, 195.
11. Bellous, "Editorial," 196.

profiles in order to see what they'd been up to since I last connected with them. I wanted to know what universities and colleges they ended up attending, which of them had moved away from our hometown, who had finally tied the knot, and which friends had become mothers and fathers.

As I read through their profiles, I was particularly struck by some friends who had written "spiritual, with no affiliation," or "more spiritual than religious" under the category of "religious views." It seemed as though some of my acquaintances believed that, as they choose which religious tradition to self-identify with, it's possible to choose whether or not they will be spiritual.[12] This is simply not true.

Although spirituality is understood and lived out differently according to various traditions, faiths, and disciplines,[13] all people are spiritual. In the words of Barbara Kimes Myers, "Spirit is a biological condition of being human."[14] Religion (and religious experiences), on the other hand, comes out of personal and social expressions of one's innate spirituality.[15] To quote Dallas Willard, "'Spiritual' is not just something we *ought* to be. It is something we *are* and cannot escape, regardless of how we may think or feel about it. It is our nature and our destiny."[16] Although neglecting or ignoring this spiritual flame can cause it to become dim, we always possess within us an innate spirituality. It is woven into the fabric of our innermost being. Regardless of religious affiliation (or lack thereof), this

12. Some people, including Jim Wallis, believe that the movement of young people claiming to be "spiritual but not religious" is quickly growing. Wallis, *Great Awakening*, 16. There is debate, however, about the validity of this view. Christian Smith has found that, contrary to popular opinion, relatively few young people in the United States see themselves as "spiritual but not religious." Smith with Snell, *Souls in Transition*, 136, 295–97. Smith with Denton, *Soul Searching*, 77–81. In Canada, however, young people seem more open to identifying themselves as spiritual outside of a religious tradition than young people in the United States. Bibby et al., *Emerging Millennials*, 163.

13. Roehlkepartain, "Exploring Scientific," 121.

14. Myers, *Young Children*, 101. Recent neurotheological and neuropsychological research has affirmed that the human brain is hardwired to receive and process spiritual experiences, thus confirming the biological innateness of spirituality. See May and Ratcliff. "Children's Spiritual Experiences" and Persinger, "Temporal Lobe."

15. Hay and Nye, *Spirit of the Child*, 25. Ratcliff, "Rituals," 10. Although spirituality and religion are distinct from one another, they are interdependent and possess a number of overlapping characteristics. See Ratcliff and Nye, "Childhood Spirituality," 477. Furthermore, spirituality can be nurtured and shaped "both within and outside of religious traditions, beliefs, and practices." Benson et al., "Spiritual Development," 206.

16. Willard, *Divine Conspiracy*, 79.

inherent quality of humankind allows us all to affirm, along with some of my Facebook friends, that we are more spiritual than religious.

Although I have already introduced the work of Robert Coles, let me offer a few more details about his research into children's spirituality. While conducting research into children's political and moral lives, Coles discovered that children conversed about spiritual matters a great deal. He believed that this spiritual realm of childhood is so important and fascinating that he set out to research and write a book that was focused entirely on children's spiritual lives. In 1990, his research was published in a groundbreaking book entitled *The Spiritual Life of Children*.

After talking with hundreds of children from different religious (and nonreligious) backgrounds, including Christianity, Islam, Judaism, and atheism, Coles concluded that children are inherently spiritual beings; they possess an innate spiritual life that "grows, changes, [and] responds constantly to the other lives that, in their sum, make up the individual we call by a name and know by a story that is all his, all hers."[17] He asserts that children are spiritual pilgrims who "march through life" on a journey to seek God, find answers, and wonder about the road ahead.[18] Coles seems amazed to discover insight into the rich and vibrant spirituality of children, as reflected in his final statement, "how young we are when we start wondering about it all, the nature of the journey and the final destination."[19] Indeed, children, like adults, are pilgrims on the spiritual journey. In the words of Don Ratcliff and Scottie May, "Spiritual aliveness knows no age barriers; the young child and aged philosopher stand on level ground."[20]

While the work of Coles initiated a shift in how people understand the spiritual lives of children, this psychologist is certainly not the only recent scholar to have gained ground in the quest to understand the spiritual dimension of childhood. Other individuals who have a hand in laying a strong foundation for exploring and defining children's spirituality include David Hay, Rebecca Nye, and Barbara Kimes Myers. Let me briefly introduce you to these individuals.

Rebecca Nye's groundbreaking doctoral research at the University of Nottingham consisted of a qualitative study exploring the spiritual

17. Coles, *Spiritual Life*, 308.

18. Ibid., 326.

19. Ibid., 335.

20. Ratcliff and May, "Identifying Children's Spirituality," 8.

realm of childhood, particularly as it was manifested in British primary school students. Her collaboration with David Hay resulted in a book entitled *The Spirit of the Child*, in which the inherent, biological nature of spirituality is unpacked.

The theory that Hay and Nye present in this book continues to be acknowledged as one of the most superb theories of children's spirituality in existence. After extensive research, Nye discovered that "children's spirituality was recognized by a distinctive property of mental activity, profound and intricate enough to be termed 'consciousness,' and remarkable for its confinement to a broadly relational, inter- and intra-personal domain."[21] Thus, Nye came to refer to spirituality as *relational consciousness*, an awareness of connection.

This spiritual aspect of the human condition is seen more clearly in children because it is a fundamental quality of human life. Some, such as Alister Hardy and David Hay, argue that it has been sustained throughout the evolutionary process because it has survival value for the species at an individual level.[22] Spirituality is necessary to humanity's survival. Without the hope, mystery, and wisdom that we derive from our relational consciousness, we would face extinction.

While Nye refers to spirituality as relational consciousness, Barbara Kimes Myers prefers to discuss the spiritual life as the process of transcendence. Transcendence, in this case, refers to the innate ability and desire to go beyond one's present self and reality—it's "the essence of who we are as humankind."[23] All children—and all people—strive to transcend their present realities, whether an impoverished girl in Southeast Asia fights to improve her living conditions or a middle-class boy in a suburb of Montréal desires to hear God's voice.

Although all people are capable of transcending the here and now, children are perhaps more apt to "grasp the reality of the transcendent and are even more open to God than many adults."[24] Again, the observation that children are more willing to experience transcendence affirms the innate biological nature of spirituality.

21. Nye, "Identifying the Core," 109.

22. Hay, "Naturalness of Relational Consciousness," 135. Alister Hardy has written extensively on the evolutionary value of spirituality, which gives strength to humankind, especially during existential crises. See Hardy, *Living Stream*.

23. Myers, *Young Children*, 101.

24. Stonehouse, *Joining Children*, 181.

Hay and Nye would agree that this desire for transcendence is a fundamental quality of spirituality, for they affirm that relational consciousness is always bound up with self-transcendence or going beyond present reality.[25] All human beings, therefore, are concerned with the transcendent, with moving beyond the here and now, for this is an inherent characteristic of the human condition. We are all born with a spiritual capacity.

Clearly, spirituality is a complex and abstract concept with no absolute or definitive definition. Rebecca Nye aptly describes spirituality as analogous to the wind: "though it might be experienced, observed and described, it cannot be 'captured.'"[26] Yet in order for us to understand it, spirituality (or at least our understanding of spirituality) needs to possess some conceptual limitations.[27] Therefore, I wish to heed the advice of Chris Boyatzis, who recommends that scholars provide their readers and audiences with their personal working definitions of children's spirituality,[28] and put forward an operational definition of spirituality that is suitable for the purposes of this book. *Spirituality, as an inherent and biological aspect of the human condition, is a sense of relational connection to a being or power that transcends the limits of ordinary, material existence.*

Different religious traditions name or describe this transcendent power differently and surely add certain nuances to this definition. Christian spirituality, for example, names the triune God as that higher power and designates the Christian community as a context through which this connection is fostered.[29] Regardless of the various nuances that religious traditions ascribe to spirituality, I believe that this definition reflects what it means to be a spiritual creature, even if it's only a partial or fuzzy reflection. "Now I know in part; then I shall know fully" (1 Cor 13:12).

---

25. Hay and Nye, *Spirit of the Child*, 157.

26. Nye, "Relational Consciousness," 58. It is interesting that the Hebrew word *ruach* and the Greek word *pneuma* can each be translated as either "wind" or "spirit."

27. Sheldrake, "What Is Spirituality?" 21.

28. Boyatzis, "Children's Spiritual Development," 48.

29. Allen, "Exploring Children's Spirituality," 11. Sheldrake, "What Is Spirituality?" 40.

SPIRITUALITY THAT IS CHRISTIAN

Although spirituality isn't synonymous with religion, it's often expressed, fostered, and developed through religious traditions. While none of us can choose to come into the world as a spiritual creature, we can each choose which religious tradition (if any) through which we will live out and cultivate this aspect of human life. I make my home within the Christian tradition, and it is through this lens that I examine and discuss the realm of spirituality and children.

At its heart, Christian spirituality identifies the triune God as the transcendent power with whom we can connect. While other religious traditions view Jesus as an important figure, Christianity claims him as the fully human and fully divine member of the triune God. Furthermore, Christianity designates the Holy Spirit as that member of the Trinity who actively engages with humanity and the world in order to help individuals connect with God, deepen their spirituality, and experience Christian formation.

Before discussing different avenues through which Christian spirituality is lived out, let me briefly explain a term that is frequently used within this tradition. Throughout the years, Christianity has often used the word *faith* to describe a conscious belief in God. One theological dictionary describes such a view when it defines faith as a "biblical word that refers both to intellectual belief and to relational trust or commitment."[30] From this perspective, which is quite pervasive in western Christianity, faith isn't an inherent quality of humankind. Rather, it is acquired through cognitive understanding and personal commitment. People often speak of a time when they "came to faith" or came to possess a proper understanding of and belief in God. While such uses of this term might appear to be satisfactory in discussions of adult theology and spirituality, they leave children (as well as mentally disabled individuals) at a deficit. Since young children, especially infants and toddlers, by virtue of their development, cannot possess certain cognitive understandings of and intentional commitment to God, such definitions of faith fail to include them. A new view is needed.

Children must have faith—why else would Jesus have said, "unless you change and become like little children, you will never enter the kingdom of heaven" (Matt 18:3)? Taking biblical scholarship and historical

---

30. Grenz et al., *Pocket Dictionary*, 50.

theology into account, Karen-Marie Yust defines faith as "a gift from God. It is neither a particular set of beliefs nor a well-developed cognitive understanding of all things spiritual. It is an act of grace in which God chooses to be in relationship with humanity."[31] According to this definition, faith is a gift bestowed by God onto all human beings—even infants.[32] It is as natural and innate as our ability to breathe. As such, faith can't be caught or transmitted. There's nothing one can do to give a child or any other person faith, for only God has the ability to bestow this precious gift on human beings.

The ideal response to the gift of faith is faithfulness. This is the aspect of faith that can be shared, developed, formed, and taught.[33] Faithfulness is the desire to express and live out one's faith in gratitude to the One who has given it. It is "a disposition that welcomes God's presence and seeks God's teaching."[34] Through intentional acts of faithfulness and human experience, our faith can grow, mature, form, and develop.

This is not to say, however, that the inexperienced and unintentional faith of a child is less real than the intentional, experienced faith of an adult. Rather, a child's faith is as whole as that of an elder. In his classic book, *Will Our Children Have Faith?*, John Westerhoff uses the metaphor of a tree to explain this concept. A small sapling, while much smaller than a full-grown tree, is as much a tree as an old redwood.[35] So the faith of a child—even that of an infant—is as whole and real as the faith of an adult. Children have real and living faith.

Three Traditions

In contemporary Christianity, spirituality and faithfulness are usually expressed through three dominant traditions: sacramental, covenantal, and conversional. First, sacramental groups include Roman Catholicism, Anglicanism, and Orthodox Churches. In these traditions, sacraments form the core of the Christian life and outwardly express an inner grace,

---

31. Yust, *Real Kids*, 6.

32. For a fascinating discussion of infant faith within the Reformed tradition, see Lusk, *Paedofaith*.

33. Yust, *Real Kids*, 18.

34. Ibid., 6.

35. Westerhoff, *Will Our Children*, 88.

which is often bestowed through the sacraments themselves.[36] Individuals first receive grace at baptism, which often occurs during infancy.

Covenantal groups, such as Presbyterian and Reformed traditions, are the second broad stream of Christianity. They see themselves as members of God's covenant. Rather than being means of grace, sacraments express this covenantal relationship between God and God's people; through baptism, infants and newcomers are welcomed into this covenantal community.[37] For both sacramental and covenantal traditions, children confirm their faithfulness to God through a form of confirmation or public profession, which often occurs when they are adolescents.

The third tradition is that of conversional groups, such as Baptists, Pentecostals, and Anabaptist traditions. Rather than receiving grace or the covenantal promise during baptism, these groups have traditionally held that people enter into a covenant and "relationship with Jesus Christ through individual repentance of sin and then acceptance of Jesus Christ as personal Savior."[38] Sometime after this conversion experience, a person should publicly display this commitment through believer's baptism, a rite of passage that parallels the sacrament of confirmation in covenantal and sacramental communities.

Formation and Transformation

While there are surely distinctive qualities to each of these traditions, they all hold to the importance of spiritual formation or transformation in the lives of their members, including children. Although definitions and strategies for growth differ from tradition to tradition, let me present overviews and working definitions of spiritual formation and transformation.

Christian spiritual *formation* refers to the process of shaping oneself according to the image of Christ and the kingdom of God that gradually occurs in the lives of people through the power of the Holy Spirit. It is an ongoing process of nurturing one's inherent spirituality and helping people to use the gifts of relationship, transcendence, and faith to connect with God and be shaped by this connection.

36. May et al., *Children Matter*, 55.
37. Ibid., 55–56.
38. Ibid., 56.

Children, in particular, can engage in spiritual formation because they are relatively new to the world and can gradually become like Christ as they grow, learn, and develop. The task of the church is to help them to be formed as "kingdom kids"—people who have never known a time when they weren't connected to the living God, following the risen Christ, and being vessels of the Holy Spirit. Writing 150 years ago, Horace Bushnell affirmed such a view of formation when he wrote, "*the child is to grow up a Christian, and never known himself* [or herself] *as being otherwise.*"[39]

Christian spiritual *transformation* refers to changes that occur as human beings are conformed to the kingdom of God and the image of Christ. While formation is a gradual process of becoming, transformation is a process of profound change from the old to the new. It can be a sudden event—such as a conversion experience—as well as an ongoing process. We experience transformation when we continually examine our lives to see how we live in ways that counter God's kingdom and Christ's image and as we seek to realign ourselves with God's purposes. For some people, this can mean they must *transform* their God concepts, worldviews, and values.

Since we are all mortal creatures, Christian spiritual formation and transformation are ongoing and can occur throughout the whole of our lifetimes. In this book, I'll use the term *trans/formation* as an inclusive reference to both formation and transformation, since both processes are essential to the spiritual life of all people.

I have offered an overview of the assumptions I hold regarding children and spirituality that form the foundation of the thoughts and ideas that I present in the following chapters. This survey of my convictions regarding children demonstrates the following: children are whole human beings and active agents who make meaning and act according to their abilities and experiences and not necessarily those imposed by outside forces; children come into the world pregnant with a spiritual capacity and, by virtue of this, they're capable of experiencing transcendence and connecting with God; children are recipients of the gift of faith and are able to live faithfully and experience spiritual trans/formation.

Let us now continue to examine the driving presuppositions of this book by examining object relations theory, which is essential for under-

---

39. Bushnell, *Christian Nurture*, 10.

standing how children, and all human beings, make meaning and come to understand God, faith communities, and the world.

THROWING AWAY THE WORLD AROUND US

Over the years, I have been involved in a wide variety of faith communities: small and large, contemplative and charismatic, thought-provoking and action-driven, sacramental, covenantal, and conversional. And each of these congregations shaped my spiritual life and the ways in which I encountered God. The charismatic churches helped to foster emotional, heartfelt connections with the Holy Spirit through heartfelt musical worship. Those that were contemplative taught me to seek God in the world around me, in the stillness of a winter's morning, the intricacy of a spring flower, and the timeless beauty of a piece of artwork. The smaller faith communities formed me into a person who values relationships and personal connections with other congregants within loving, respectful environments. In these churches, every person can claim his or her voice as the congregation members gather together and scatter like seeds sprouting up God's vision for the world. And the congregations that were marked by thought-provoking and passionate sermons have made me into a person who knows and appreciates the trans/formative power of good preaching.

These examples from the many faith communities of which I have been a part demonstrate that our environments profoundly affect our spiritual experiences. As we engage in the world around us—both inside and outside of faith communities—we make meaning of the world and our experiences within it.

This is as true for children as it is for adults. Perhaps this holds even more truth for children, since their relative lack of experience in the world means that they're often seeing, feeling, smelling, hearing, touching, and sensing things—as well as making meaning of them—for the first time. And in the process, they're forming key opinions and views about the people, places, and objects in their lives, ideas that can stay with them for years to come. Through making sense of the people and places that they interact with at church, home, and elsewhere, children come to see these faces and spaces as welcoming or inhospitable, safe and secure or fraught with danger, spiritually nurturing or cold and unfit for experiencing transcendence.

Claims about the ways in which people make meaning of the world around them can fall under the realm of object relations theory, which derives from the work of Sigmund Freud, Donald W. Winnicott, and Ana-Maria Rizzuto, among others. For the remainder of this chapter, I'll finish laying the foundation with a rudimentary discussion of the theory of object relations in order to explain how human beings make meaning of the world and their experiences within it. Welcome to Object Relations 101.

Defining object relations is a daunting if not impossible task, for there isn't a single, all-encompassing definition of this theory. Rather, "It is the general term for a collection of psychoanalytic theories . . . that focus on the impact of early relationships with significant others (especially parents) on personal and interpersonal development."[40] In lay terminology, object relations deals with how people's relationships and interactions with significant people, places, and objects impact their understanding, development, and ways of making meaning. Without attempting to define object relations theory, let me paint a picture of this concept using broad brush strokes.

As new human beings, infants cannot differentiate themselves from the world around them—they're completely embedded in their surrounding environments. Their agency and ability to make meaning is expressed through this embeddedness, in which they perceive everything around them as extensions of themselves. Infants see Mommy, Daddy, older siblings, toys, and bottles as parts of themselves.

As they grow, children gradually gain the ability to differentiate between themselves and the other. Mommy and the stuffed doll are no longer seen as extensions of oneself, but as objects unto themselves. Through this process of differentiation, which continues throughout one's lifetime, human beings come to have relationships with various objects in the world and know about these relationships.[41] "Object relations theory is the study of these internal and external relationships in healthy children and adults."[42]

The etymology of the word *object* sheds some light on this process of differentiation and on the theory of object relations in general. The root of this word, *ject*, conveys a sense of movement, more specifically,

40. Rubin, "Psychoanalytic Treatment," 94.

41. Hamilton, *Self and Others*, 3.

42. Ibid., 4.

a throwing motion.[43] The verb *eject*, which shares the same root, speaks of movement, such as ejecting a disc from a Blu-ray player.[44] Another example is the verb *project*, which implies a propelling movement, such as a video projector that casts (or throws) images from a filmstrip onto a large screen. When the prefix *ob* is added to the base, the word conveys a sense of "thrown from" or "thrown away from."[45] Therefore, the word *object* refers to something that has been thrown from oneself and is now separate from oneself—the other to which the self relates.[46] When an infant recognizes a stuffed doll as an entity distinct from herself, she can now see that the doll is an object separate from who she is; it's been "thrown away" from the child. *Object* refers to what is not internal to oneself; it refers to "a person or thing in an individual's external environment which becomes internally or psychologically significant."[47]

With this understanding in mind, Robert Kegan supposes that object relating "might be expected to have to do with our relations to that which some motion has made separate or distinct from us, our relations to that which has been thrown from us, or the experience of this throwing itself."[48] Our relationships with objects in our environments add up over time and work together to structure our mind and form the ways in which we relate to and interact with the world.[49]

What a mouthful! Clearly, object relations isn't an easy concept to understand and explain. Speaking broadly, this theory examines how human beings use our relations with external people, places, and objects to create inner structures that shape our behaviors, our understandings of the world, and our relationships with other people.[50] Josephine Klein states that object relations is about "our relations to the 'objects'—the people and things—to which we are attached and which give meaning to our lives."[51] This process affects human beings from the beginning of life.

43. Kegan, *Evolving Self*, 76.

44. The premise for this analogy is taken from Bellous, *Educating Faith*, 72.

45. Bellous, *Educating Faith*, 72.

46. St. Clair, *Object Relations and Self Psychology*, 5.

47. St. Clair, *Human Relationships*, 7.

48. Kegan, *Evolving Self*, 76.

49. St. Clair, *Human Relationships*, 7.

50. R. Klein, *Object Relations and Family Process*, 17. St. Clair, *Human Relationships*, 8.

51. J. Klein, *Our Need for Others*, xv.

When it comes to human spirituality and faith, object relations theory matters. It's at the core of the spiritual life.[52] Spirituality and meaning making are profoundly affected by the people, places, and things that make up one's environment. The way we conceptualize God, worship, pray, and engage in spiritual trans/formation is influenced by the world around us. To study how church environments affect children is to study the relations that exist between congregations and the children that perceive them. It's a pursuit that cuts to the heart of a child's faith and spirituality.

Places and Spaces

Places, as collections of objects, are relevant to conversations about children's spirituality and object relations. As I use them in this book, places and spaces refer to the physical surroundings that children interact with at their homes and churches, including the various items and objects that are part of these environments. Since one's physical surroundings are "thrown away" from the self, places are objects and affect the people who interact with and occupy them.

Within church buildings (including other spaces where Christian communities meet), it's not uncommon for children to occupy spaces removed from the wider faith community. Whether or not they are present for parts of Sunday services, it's fairly normal for children to be separated from the wider congregation and instructed in places set aside for them. Such spaces—those occupied by the church's children—come in all shapes and sizes. While some may resemble school classrooms, others are reminiscent of jungle-gyms. Some spaces look like ornate chapels, while others seem like storage rooms. Whatever their design or décor, these places and spaces are given meaning by children in profound ways, according to object relations theory.

Every aspect of a space—from the colors of the walls to the odors received by the nose—come together to speak to those within it.[53] Children and adults alike can gather a great deal of information by observing and analyzing a room or space. They can learn about the theology, practices, and values of those who own the space or have designed and created it. For example, if a room is well-kept, clean, and organized,

52. Bellous, *Educating Faith*, 27.
53. Berryman, *Godly Play*, 80.

it demonstrates that those who own the room are diligent in their care for it and probably care for the children who use it. On the other hand, a room that has paint peeling from the walls, cobwebs forming in the corners, and objects strewn about the floor tells us that the owners care little for this space. The children who spend time in this room may also sense that they aren't cared for.

Take some time to reflect on the space that you currently find yourself in. How does it make you feel? What do you notice about it? What does it tell you about the people who created it, own it, and maintain it? You may also want to ask these questions about different places in your home, church building, or another place that's special to you. Places and spaces convey a great deal of information to those who observe and occupy them. This information offers unspoken messages, or an implicit curriculum, to those who are in these spaces.[54]

Children in particular are sensitive to spaces that don't speak of safety, inclusivity, hospitality, and the supernatural. They need environments that provide them with a sense of fit and touch them at a spiritual level. It's unfortunate, then, that many churches use inappropriate or less-than-desirable space for children. Rather than creating sacred spaces and places in which children are included and given opportunities to experience God, some churches provide them with spaces that resemble school classrooms, playgrounds, or even offices. One church near my home advertises the space for their children's ministry—which resembles a large McDonald's Playland—by saying "It's like going to the park, but it's indoors!" While the leaders of this church certainly mean well, they don't appear to believe, as I do, that the task of churches is to offer children environments that are set aside as sacred spaces—places where God can be readily perceived and experienced. This is also the task of parents and families who wish to help their children grow up with profound experiences and personal knowledge of God.

A church building should be a special place created to help people to authentically worship God. It's a place that declares spoken and unspoken messages about those who gather together in the space. This must be taken into account when designing and decorating churches.

54. Elliot Eisner refers to the implicit curriculum as "what [a school] teaches because of the kind of place it is.... And because [features of the implicit curriculum] are salient and pervasive features of schooling, what they teach may be among the most important lessons a child learns." Eisner, *Educational Imagination*, 97.

More so than adults, children use all their senses to make meaning of the world around them. And from a young age, they come to understand the world by taking ideas and messages from their surroundings.[55] Aspects of a space that are easily ignored by adults can be readily perceived by children. This also applies at a spiritual level—the character of a space can significantly affect whether or not a child experiences transcendence or senses God's presence.

I grew up attending Holy Redeemer Church in Sudbury, Ontario. Every Sunday, my family and I would pile into the car and head over to this quaint church that sat across from a lake. As I mentioned in the introduction, I loved sitting in the sanctuary, looking around at the symbolism and watching the rituals of the Mass unfold around me. When I was a young child, I always wanted to sit in the front row of the church, close to the action and the elements that spoke of God. But when I turned around and saw the balcony, the front row just didn't do it for me anymore. Up in the balcony, I had a bird's-eye view and I found myself better able to take in all that was happening in the church. Holy Redeemer was a space created to speak of God, to send messages about the people in the building, and to foster personal connections with the transcendent. I still remember the sights, sounds, smells, tastes, and feelings that I had in that building. Clearly, the space was infused with transcendental characteristics that helped me to have first-hand encounters with God and set me on a path to know God.

Children "sense and respond to the environment of the church."[56] When explicit, voiced theologies or ideas that are presented to children conflict with the implicit, unspoken messages that young people receive from their environments, children can become confused, frustrated, and feel excluded. These negative feelings can cause them to close themselves off from transcendence and encountering God.[57] The four scholars who authored the book *Children Matter* state this quite clearly: "*the preparation of the space or environment profoundly affects the learning that takes*

---

55. Yust, "Creating a Spiritual World," 28. A recent study discovered that even in the womb, human fetuses pick up on and memorize the sounds that they hear, which in turn affects the melodies of infants' cries. Mampe et al., "Newborns' Cry."

56. May et al., *Children Matter*, 210.

57. Such frustration was clearly demonstrated by Caleb, a boy who participated in the research on which this book is based. See pages 62–63 in chapter 3.

place."[58] And children's learning and meaning making can structure how they understand God and the world for years to come.

In his classic book about children, John Westerhoff stated that the "space we create has tremendous influence on us."[59] What does this mean for those who create and adapt the spaces that are occupied by children, whether at church, home, or somewhere else altogether? It reminds us of the importance of continually investigating the unspoken and implicit messages that are offered by spaces and examining how children react to such places. By talking with thirteen children from three congregations that use places and spaces in different ways, I was able to gain insight into how children's spiritual experiences are affected by spaces. While the study of place and environment permeates this book, it's important to remember the great effects that environments can have on a child's spiritual life. Exploring how places affect children and their experiences with God is a vital task for all who wish to welcome and nurture children.

Faces

While object relations deals with the relationships between human beings and place, it also examines our relationships with other people. Some theorists so strongly emphasize these latter relations that they argue that the "'objects' in object relations are human beings."[60] Such a view of this theory affirms what a young girl once succinctly told me: "People are things." As objects, people with whom children come into contact affect their spiritual experiences. Whether parents, babysitters, or Sunday school teachers, the individuals children interact with at churches can profoundly influence their spirituality, spiritual trans/formation, and experiences with God.

In many congregations, children's programs function simultaneously to Sunday services. Such age-segregated styles of ministry often result in adults and children occupying different places. This being the case, going to church and worshipping God can hardly be considered a family event. It would be as if parents enjoyed a meal at the dinner table while their children learned to cook in the basement. Although

---

58. May et al., *Children Matter*, 252.

59. Westerhoff, *Will Our Children*, 140.

60. Cashdan, *Object Relations Therapy*, 3.

congregations may believe that it's in the best interest of children to have separate programs, it's vital for children to be a part of the wider faith community by attending worship services and engaging in trans/formative practices. This is a topic that I'll turn to in chapter 5.

Furthermore, it is broadly recognized that parents have a unique and prominent influence on the spiritual lives of their children, especially regarding their concepts of God.[61] Therefore, it's beneficial for children to worship alongside their parents, witnessing their words and actions as they celebrate and worship with the wider faith community. Some who would affirm this argue that the church is less than God has intended it to be when children are excluded from the core practices that define its life.[62] With these ideas in mind, it could be counterproductive for churches to exclude children from their worship services and from the wider community of faith.

Since many children participate in church programs held simultaneously to worship services, they don't typically encounter large numbers of adults at their faith communities. Rather, many young people interact with their peers and a select group of leaders, children's ministers, and volunteers responsible for teaching and leading them during these programs. These adults, as living objects, have relationships with children and can greatly affect how young people experience God and engage in trans/formation.

Studying the relations between children and the places and people that they encounter in congregations is of profound importance; these relationships can greatly influence their spirituality and experiences with God. Since, as Michael St. Clair says, "Relationships and events that take place during development can dramatically shape the individual's religious experience and relationship to God and the sacred,"[63] it's important to examine environments in order to understand how pastors, educators, and parents can create positive, inclusive spaces that welcome and nurture all children.

61. See Rizzuto, *Birth of the Living God.*

62. May et al., *Children Matter*, 143.

63. St. Clair, *Human Relationships*, 12.

Rather than seeing children as blank slates, I believe that young people, as spiritual, faith-filled agents and learners, continually make meaning of the world around them, including the people and places with which they interact. As such, children possess knowledge and perspectives that are valuable and worthy of investigation. Since listening to young people "is central to recognizing and respecting their worth as human beings,"[64] it is to this topic that we now turn.

---

64. Roberts, "Listening to Children," 264.

❧ 2

Examining the Diamond

Practices for Hearing Children's Voices

ON A COLD JANUARY day, I stepped out of my basement apartment
and made my way to a local shopping district. I had one thing on
my list: an engagement ring for my girlfriend. I hoped to find a ring with
the perfect juxtaposition of classic simplicity and unique flair. At a small
jewelry store, I found what I'd been looking for—a single round diamond
set into an unadorned white gold band. Clearly, the ring was classic in
its style. It wasn't until I looked closely at the diamond that I realized
what made this ring somewhat unique. While standard round diamonds
have fifty-eight facets cut into them, this one had one hundred facets. It
may have looked like a regular diamond at first sight, but on closer in-
spection, the extra forty-two facets caused it to reflect more light and so
sparkle brighter than some other diamonds. This was a perfect symbol
for my wife-to-be—she was classic and timeless, but when you look a
little closer and get to know her, you start to see just what makes her so
brilliant and unique.

While this diamond is analogous to my wife, it's also a fitting metaphor for studying children's spirituality. To see the many facets of a diamond, we need to observe it from several angles. So it is with exploring
the spiritual dimension of childhood. The nature of spirituality and the
phenomenon of childhood combine to make such a task rather challenging. Anyone wanting to explore the spiritual lives of children must
have multiple methods and perspectives in place to guide them in the
research process. Seasoned researchers like Don Ratcliff know that when
it comes to children's spirituality, having "multiple views helps in the

understanding of the whole."[1] Although adequately hearing children's voices can be challenging, it's an essential practice for congregations, organizations, and individuals who wish to nurture and encourage children along their spiritual journeys.

At the end of the previous chapter, I put forth my belief that listening to children and learning about their knowledge, perspectives, and worldviews is vital to respecting them as whole human beings. Additionally, I believe that effective ministry with children begins with learning about their views, the meaning that they make. Adults, therefore, should take the time and effort to listen to the children around them in order to gain a sense of how they feel about God, church, and the world in which they live. In the words of Cathy Stonehouse and Scottie May, authors of *Listening to Children on the Spiritual Journey*, "Listening to children is a crucial part of our relationship with them. It brings pleasure, helps us know what the child needs, and can even teach us valuable lessons."[2] Ministry *with* children, ministry that values young people as spiritual pilgrims, involves listening to them on the spiritual journey.

In this chapter I present the different methods I used in my research to hear children speak about their spirituality and their experiences with God. Although not all of these practices and methods may be suitable for every context, those who wish to hear and understand the children in their ministries can benefit from knowing how another person has done so. Whether you're a pastor, parent, teacher, or researcher, the following pages will equip you to learn, as Jesus did some 2000 years ago, from the children in your midst. After all, "the kingdom of God belongs to such as these" (Matt 10:14).[3]

YOUNG FRIENDS ON THE SPIRITUAL JOURNEY

Before getting to the methods I used to gain insight into children's spiritual lives, I want to introduce readers to the children who were part of my research. For six months, I conducted a qualitative research project with thirteen children between the ages of seven and ten in order to gain a window into their encounters with God and their experiences at their congregations. I met with them in small groups to hear them tell

1. Ratcliff, "Beginnings," 2.

2. Stonehouse and May, *Listening to Children*, 11.

3. To more fully understand what Jesus was attempting to teach his followers by placing a child in the midst, see Csinos, "Biblical Theme," 104–6.

their stories about church, home, family, and God. They spoke about the special places where they went to meet God and about the people they admired. Since their stories are at the core of this book, it is important to have a sense of these thirteen children and their congregations.[4]

Each of the three faith communities involved in my research was intentionally chosen based on its differences and similarities to the other two. All three churches are located in the same geographical region and fall within the Protestant theological tradition, although two congregations are conversional and the third is covenantal in its tradition. In each church, the children gather at the beginning of services for large-group teaching or song time and are subsequently separated into different age-based groups. Such rotational, pragmatic-participatory models, which focus on practical lessons that engage children through various related activities, have become quite widespread in Protestant churches, especially those of an evangelical flavor.[5] Several popular curricula and resources, like those published by Promiseland (out of Willow Creek Community Church) and Group Publishing, reflect this approach to ministry. Let me briefly describe each congregation and the children who took part in my research.

Northview Community Church

Northview Community Church is a two-decade-old congregation with a weekly attendance of over 1,100 people, 300 of whom are children under the age of twelve. This independent Baptist church values "exalting God, embracing others, evangelizing seekers, and equipping followers,"[6] and lives out these values through seeker-sensitive teaching in a "friendly and casual atmosphere."[7] Looking back to the three broad streams of Christianity discussed in chapter 1, it is safe to say that Northview falls within the conversional tradition.

Recently, this community built a new structure on the northwest perimeter of its city. The building, which sits on a property of thirty three acres, has a massive foyer featuring enormous windows overlooking an

---

4. To maintain confidentiality, each person and congregation involved in my research has been given a pseudonym.

5. For more information on this model of children's ministry, see Graves, "Pragmatic-Participatory."

6. This quotation is taken from the website of Northview Community Church.

7. Taken from the website of Northview Community Church.

in-ground water fountain. This foyer leads to the sanctuary, which was actually built as a gymnasium. Each week, the congregation—mainly consisting of young families—gathers under basketball nets and in front of a stage draped with black cloths for contemporary worship music and "relevant and engaging teaching."[8] The children meet in whatever room is available in the building, from the boardroom to a bigger, generic room featuring a stage for a children's worship band. Virtually no Christian symbolism is found in this building, which is characterized by neutral colors and tones.

Three children from Northview were part of my research sample. Caleb, a quiet nine-year-old boy, had, until a few years ago, lived in Asia with his sister and parents, who served as missionaries. Abigail, a nine-year-old girl who was homeschooled by her parents, was another participant. Ben, the third child from this church, was a humorous and energetic seven-year-old who loved attending the focus group conversations. He and his family had been coming to Northview for several years.

Townsend Baptist Church

Townsend Baptist Church is found on the southeast corner of its city. Founded in the late 1960s, this conversional church (affiliated with the Fellowship of Evangelical Baptist Churches) has blossomed into one of the region's largest congregations. According to its website, "Thirty-five years after [the] first service . . . over 1,500 people call Townsend home."[9] Over 350 children attend this church's weekly programs that seek to foster a "kid-munity"[10] focused on Townsend's six foundations: belonging, worshipping, caring, learning, serving, and reaching.[11]

The congregation meets in a sizeable facility built in three phases, the most recent of which was completed in 2003. On the main floor is a foyer with glass walls facing the parking lot, a roomy library, offices, and several nursery and toddler rooms. The heart of the church is its worship center, a sloped auditorium that seats 600 people. The pews are arranged in a semi-circular manner, facing a multi-leveled platform

---

8. Taken from the website of Northview Community Church.

9. This quotation was taken from the website of Townsend Baptist Church.

10. On Townsend's website, they describe their Sunday children's programs as "an interactive 'kid-munity.'"

11. Taken from the website of Townsend Baptist Church.

and two looming projection screens. The lower level of the building is dedicated to children's ministry and contains a gymnasium, where the children meet for large-group sessions, surrounded by several class-rooms of varying sizes. With entrances to the building on both levels, it's possible that some adults and children never interact with one another while they're at church. Although Townsend's worship center is more traditional than Northview's, the entire building is fairly contemporary and contains little Christian symbolism.

Five children from Townsend participated in my research, the youngest of whom was Laurie, an eight-year-old girl who appeared timid at first. Before long, however, she became comfortable with the group and eagerly shared her ideas and experiences. Laurie's older sister, Keira, was an energetic and imaginative ten-year-old who enjoyed mak-ing people laugh. Nine-year-old Megan was an only child who'd been attending Townsend for about four years and, since first coming to the congregation, she and her family had become quite involved in the life of this church. Two brothers met with me on Wednesday mornings. Nicholas was a nine-year-old boy who proved willing to participate in the focus groups, despite being nervous about talking with people. His eight-year-old brother, Owen, seemed shy and timid, but became com-fortable with the research process as time progressed.

Lawrence Park Presbyterian Church

Contrasting Northview and Townsend is Lawrence Park Presbyterian Church, a 150-year-old downtown parish that finds its home within the covenantal tradition. This church, which was at one time the biggest Presbyterian congregation in the country, has resided in its enormous maze-like building since the early 1900s. While it's no longer the nation's largest Presbyterian parish, its weekly attendance of 600 is impressive, especially for a mainline church. The congregation is dominated by people in middle adulthood and their senior years, many of whom have been members for most of their lives. Children make up less than 14 percent of the congregation.[12]

Lawrence Park's sanctuary is a large structure with concentric curved pews on the main and gallery levels. The pulpit features a massive pipe organ embedded in dark wood and elevated levels for the minister,

---

12. This information is from the website of Lawrence Park Presbyterian Church.

pulpit, and choir. The sanctuary is decorated with flags, banners, colors reflecting the church year, and an array of stained glass windows depicting saints and the mission of the church. The liturgy follows the Book of Common Worship and wraps up with a children's time, when the children gather in the front pews for a lesson from the minister. In general, Lawrence Park has an intergenerational approach to church and intentionally includes children in special programs, intergenerational events, and portions of the worship service.[13]

During their rotational Sunday school, children can be found throughout the building. They begin in the chapel, the church's original sanctuary featuring dark wood and stained glass windows, and disperse throughout the building after their gathering time. Some file to the Potter's House, a room depicting the land on which Jesus walked. Others go to the Odeon, a small theatre featuring movie-style seating and dark walls decorated with stars. Children also are found in a hall that looks like Solomon's Temple, complete with gold pillars. Clearly, Lawrence Park has created spaces that speak of God and depict the spiritual life of the faith community. This is quite different from the generic classrooms of Townsend and Northview.

Five children from this faith community were involved in my sample. The oldest was ten-year-old Freddy, who seemed to be a born leader. His brother, Gordon, was a quiet eight-year-old who looked up to Freddy and loved playing games and eating delicious snacks with his friends at church. Another set of brothers was involved in the Lawrence Park group. The youngest was Ian, a seven-year-old who didn't seem to follow his elder brother's example as willingly as Gordon did. Ian's brother was Houston, a ten-year-old self-proclaimed perfectionist who loved drama, music, and the arts. The fifth child involved was Juliet, a friendly and self-assured ten-year-old girl who lived with her mother, step-father, and two older step-siblings.

These thirteen children were the heart of my research and are the soul of this book. Without their generosity and honesty in sharing their spiritual lives, this book wouldn't exist. Throughout the remaining chapters, I draw on their experiences as I put forth strategies and tactics

---

13. Holly Allen cites six key forms of intergenerational church activities, three of which are practiced by Lawrence Park. See Allen, "Nurturing Children's Spirituality in Intergenerational," 267–68.

for including all children, ever grateful and respectful of the children, parents, and congregations that aided me in this process.

HAVING EARS TO HEAR

I began this chapter by stating that explorations into the spiritual lives of children require multiple methods of data acquisition. *"The more sources of information an adult has about a child, the more likely that the adult is to receive the child's messages properly."*[14] A multi-method, "mosaic" approach allows children with various interests and skills to become involved in the process and it offers those seeking understanding a more holistic picture of their spiritual lives.[15] It helps adults to have "ears to hear" the voices of children.

For my research, I made use of several qualitative methods: semi-structured focus groups with children, social mapping exercises, drawing, interviews with parents, and photographic documentation. These ways of doing exploratory research *with* children allow the young participants to have legitimate voices in the process and lead to more accurate and valid results.[16]

Although qualitative approaches to hearing children's voices can be affected by personal biases and usually include far fewer participants than quantitative research methods, they can also prove to be more effective than quantitative methods for accurately studying children's spirituality and hearing their voices. While the latter "provides precision . . . its results, while technically accurate, may miss the point of a child's behavior."[17] Since children often have limited vocabulary and can have trouble expressing themselves, those wishing to gain a clear window into their spiritual lives do well to use methods that are subjective, holistic, and anthropological, with the goal of accurately understanding their views.[18] Furthermore, the relative lack of control in qualitative research allows the children to better assume the role of teacher, rather than seeing the adult as an instructor or authority figure, which can hinder their willingness to honestly express themselves.

14. Garbarino et al., *What Children*, 15.

15. See Clark, "Mosaic Approach."

16. Lloyd-Smith and Tarr, "Researching Children's Perspectives," 60–62. Garbarino et al., *What Children*, 15.

17. Garbarino et al., *What Children*, 149–50.

18. Ratcliff, "Qualitative Research."

In choosing to use qualitative research methods, I sacrificed a much larger sample of people for more detailed information and more personal connections with each child. This is why my sample consisted of only thirteen children. With all the interview planning, in-depth focus groups, exercises, transcribing, and data analysis, having even a few more children would have necessitated 27-hour days and 35-day months. My research with this small group of thirteen young people offered me more detailed and in-depth glimpses into their lives. While they are surely not representative of all children in all contexts, much of what they shared with me was consistent with what I (and my colleagues) have seen and experienced with other children.

Speaking from experience, Nye explains why qualitative methods are well-suited for research with children: "The quantitative approach too easily lends itself to becoming numbers about numbers, which for discussing matters of faith and the numinous is a fate even worse than when theology becomes merely words about words. As a relatively new field, and as one unanimously regarded as complex, ambiguous, and surprising, children's spirituality is not adequately delineated to tolerate number crunching. People need the stories, the personal, the descriptions, the creative analyses."[19] Another seasoned researcher, David Elkind, interviewed hundreds of children from different religious backgrounds and his research demonstrates that children's anecdotes and stories provide valuable information about their religious and spiritual experiences and views.[20] From children's narratives and other exercises, theories are produced from the ground up and better reflect the voices and experiences of young people.[21] For all these reasons, examining the spirituality of children is an undertaking that requires qualitative research methods.

Let me present the methods that I used in my exploration of the spiritual lives of thirteen children. The following pages describe how I gathered the information in this book; they are also meant to encourage and assist readers who seek to hear the voices of the children in their midst.

---

19. Nye, "Christian Perspectives," 105.

20. Elkind, *Sympathetic Understanding*, 151–54.

21. Greig, et al., *Doing Research*, 51.

Let's Get Together: Semi-Structured Focus Groups

The best way to find out about someone is to get to know him or her on a personal level. And to get to know people, we need to talk with them, to discover what's important to them, who they are, and how they understand and experience the world around them. Having conversations with the children in our lives helps us to know them in more personal and accurate ways. I've found that one way to have such conversations is to talk with children and listen to them as they converse with one another.

Each of the thirteen young pilgrims who were part of my research met with me and my research assistant for a total of five focus group discussions, with as few as one and as many as five children present, depending on their availability. Every child in each focus group attended the same congregation. Except in a few special circumstances, all of the meetings took place at the children's churches. This choice of location was an important part of the process, for places that children are familiar with "are apt to elicit the most meaningful communications with children."[22] Since the children were familiar with their churches, they didn't need to acclimatize themselves to a new environment and my relationship with each child was eased.[23]

During each of these focus group conversations, I fostered discussion by asking open-ended questions and allowing the children time to respond and talk about their thoughts with one another. When exploring the experiences of children through qualitative research, open-ended questions are preferable because children "respond better to open, indirect questions, which leave a substantial (but not infinite) range for response."[24] In conducting the interviews in this way, I was able to create an environment in which the children could express themselves and I empowered them to become active members of the research process. Both of these elements of the focus groups were fundamental strategies of eliciting information about children's inner experiences.[25]

During the focus group meetings, I minimized any socially-perceived grown-up roles by taking on what Nancy Mandell refers to as

---

22. Garbarino et al., *What Children*, 106.

23. Nesbitt, "Researching," 143.

24. Garbarino et al., *What Children*, 188.

25. Hill, "Ethical Considerations," 63.

the "least-adult role"[26] and offering the children a measure of freedom to guide the conversations and activities. Rather than being told exactly how meetings would proceed, the children could decide on what we discussed and when we did various activities. Qualitative researchers who study children know the value of giving them a degree of freedom: "When children become too conscious of their dependency on adults they become less spontaneous and more wary of factors in the situation that may threaten their security. Feeling some sense of control in the situation allows them to attend to the purpose of the interview."[27]

Throughout the interviews, I consistently reminded the children that I wasn't assuming the role of pastor or teacher. I was the student, the learner, and they were my teachers who helped to direct the learning process. This is a vital component of learning about the inner lives of children. While some of my young conversation partners preferred to simply answer my open-ended questions, others enjoyed the liberty I offered to them and dialogued with each other about their experiences in transparent manners. In this way, "Children become the instructors and we, as researchers, become the pupils."[28] Robert Coles emphasized this style of conversational, participant-led research. In his words, "I let the children know as clearly as possible, and as often as necessary, what it is I am trying to learn, how they can help me."[29] Those wishing to have ears to hear children communicate about their spiritual lives ought to do likewise.

As the pupil, I didn't relinquish all control during the focus groups. Although I was able to build a rapport with most of the children and offer them some control of the process, I sometimes found myself having to gently guide their conversations in order to hear them speak about topics that were pertinent to my research questions. Sometimes the children didn't run with the freedom that I offered to them, so I engaged them in conversation by asking open-ended questions, ever cautious not to transform the focus group conversations into oral surveys. Throughout the entire process, my intention was to gently guide the children as they spoke with one another about their encounters with God and their experiences at their congregations.

26. Mandell, "Least-Adult Role."

27. Garbarino et al., *What Children*, 175.

28. Emond, "Ethnographic Research Methods," 124.

29. Coles, *Spiritual Life*, 27.

As with all qualitative research with children, rapport with each participant is essential for accurately hearing their voices. You can't just expect children to open up to complete strangers (and I wouldn't want to encourage children to do so). To build relationships with my thirteen young friends, we spent time talking with one another about our personal lives. I learned about their favorite foods, television shows, movies, and sports. Some of the girls helped me hone my French-speaking skills as they told me about their French immersion schools. Nicholas and Owen showed me how to play the latest Nintendo DS video games.

Relationships are two-way streets. As I learned about the children, I needed to spend time telling them about who I was. I shared with them the fact that I was a graduate student and, at the time the focus groups began, I was also a children's pastor. This helped me to become an insider to their Christian church culture. "All human communities have a perspective on life, a philosophy for living that underlies behavior."[30] By being able to see me as an insider, the children could become more open and honest about experiences within this culture. Throughout the interviews, I hoped that they came to know me just as I came to know them.

Having a female research assistant at the focus groups also helped me to build rapport, for women can be more effective at connecting with children on a personal level and are often perceived as less threatening.[31]

Meeting at the children's churches, offering the children control, becoming open with the children, and having a female assistant were all essential elements of the focus group conversation process. Through these practices, I was able to provide what Nye believes is vital for research with children: "a context of protected time and a sense of 'safe enough' space, and of course relationships, [which are] an essential piece of equipment for studying Christian spirituality."[32] These elements of the focus groups gave me ears to hear their stories, experiences, and opinions.

30. Garbarino et al., *What Children*, 103.
31. Holmes, *Fieldwork*, 61.
32. Nye, "Christian Perspectives," 100.

Becoming Cartographers through Social Mapping

While focus group discussions provide a way to connect with children through verbal communication, it's important to use other methods of hearing their voices as well. Some of the most effective methods aid us in hearing their nonverbal voices.

One way of visually connecting with children is through social mapping exercises, which are especially useful in helping to understand children's geographical views. Social mapping, as a form of qualitative research, is relatively new and unexplored. However, in studying children in post-genocide Rwanda, Angela Veale discovered that social maps act as descriptive and analytical tools. They're descriptive in that they show the child's perspective of the geographical area being depicted. They are analytical in that they "generated visual data, a 'map' of the community that could be analyzed through determining the features and people that were included and also those that were excluded."[33] By having the children perform social mapping exercises, my intent was to discover some insight into their views of the social demographics of their church's Sunday services.

Through social mapping, children become cartographers—those who make maps. I gave each child a map of his or her church and two sets of small plastic pieces. Each set of pieces was a different color. I asked the children to designate one color to represent children and the other to represent adults and to place the pieces on their maps in ways that depicted where children and adults spend time at their church on Sunday mornings.[34] For example, if a child thought that many adults spend time in the library, then she would place a number of pieces that represent adults on the library area of the map. When these social maps were completed, I briefly discussed each one with the respective child, having them explain why they placed their pieces where they did. After taking pictures of these maps, I asked the children to change them in any way that would reflect where they would prefer adults and children to reside on Sunday mornings. Some children didn't want to change anything, while others wiped the slate clean and created completely different social maps. I then photographed and discussed these second maps with the children.

33. Veale, "Creative Methodologies," 259.

34. I intentionally avoided telling the children what I considered a "child" and an "adult," leaving them to make such designations for themselves.

After finishing this exercise, each child had created two social maps—one *descriptive*, depicting his or her views of where people spend time during church services, and one *prescriptive*, showing where he or she would prefer people to spend this time. I was then able to compare these two maps, along with the children's comments about them, which allowed me to see their views of the places that children and adults inhabit at their churches versus where they wish people at their churches would spend time.

Making the Inner Self Visible through Children's Artwork

I've already mentioned that children, due to their age and development, often lack an adequate vocabulary for speaking of their spiritual experiences. They certainly have spiritual experiences; they just can't always describe them. This being the case, many researchers find it helpful to have children draw pictures related to issues and topics that one wishes to explore.[35] As a universal pictorial language, drawing "makes a portion of the inner self visible."[36]

In his research with young people from across the globe, Coles has often asked children to draw pictures of God, heaven, church, or biblical characters. This helps them to more holistically and accurately express themselves and disclose their experiences and perceptions. Others, like Klepsch and Logie, also know the value of children's drawings, for drawings "seem to be able to plumb the inner depths of a person and uncover some of the otherwise inaccessible inside information."[37]

While the drawings themselves provide information, a wealth of data can be gathered through the child's verbalization about their artwork both during the drawing process and after they create their pictures.[38] The concrete experience of drawing sprouts new insights in the imagination of the child that may not have otherwise been discussed or portrayed. Therefore, it can be helpful to have children verbally reflect on their drawings and on the act of creating their artwork. Drawings not

35. Researchers who have used children's drawings to study children's spirituality include Robert Coles (*Spiritual Life*), Sofia Cavalletti (*Religious Potential*), David Heller (*Children's God*), Karen Crozier and Elizabeth Conde-Frazier ("Narrative of Children's Spirituality"), and Dana Hood ("Six Children").

36. Klepsch and Logie, *Children Draw*, 6.

37. Ibid., 11.

38. Boyatzis and Newman, "How Shall We Study," 172–73.

only provide people with data about the picture; they also yield information about the children's perceptions and interpretations about the drawing and the ideas conveyed in the picture.

Dana Hood believes that drawing pictures helps children to articulate their concepts and ideas by giving them a context through which they can express themselves. Children's verbalizations while drawing offer valuable insight into their perceptions and experiences, since drawings are only partial representations of their views. After all, they can only use symbols and techniques available to them through knowledge, experience, and talent. With my lack of drawing skills, it would be difficult for me to accurately represent myself without also speaking about what I was creating. Since children's drawings "are often metaphors to represent ideas,"[39] having children discuss their pictures as they draw helps to gain a more holistic and accurate sense of what they are saying through artwork. Drawing and speaking work together.

During the third set of focus groups, the children drew pictures of people who help them know God or feel close to God, as well as places where they experience God.[40] Each child was given a blank sheet of white paper and chose the medium he or she wanted to work with: crayons, pencils, markers, paints, or colored pencils. Some children hurried right to the paints while others were content to make simple pencil drawings. They were given as much time as they needed. It's important not to rush children as they draw so that they have the freedom to work at their own pace and the time to reflect on their artwork.

Since up to five children were drawing at one time, there was no way for me to talk with each one of them for the entire time that he or she drew. Without a few clones of myself, all that I was able to do was spend a few moments with each young artist. Afterwards, we gathered as a group for the children to share their pictures with one another. Presenting and chatting about the drawings proved to be a fruitful method of learning about the children's spiritual experiences, for group discussions about the people and places in the drawings often ensued.

39. Hood, "Six Children," 245.

40. Due to time constraints, the children from Lawrence Park and the girls from Townsend were not able to draw a picture of a place where they feel close to God or experience God. Some, however, incorporated images of places into the first drawing. These children adequately addressed places where they feel close to God through their photographs and conversations.

"Say Cheese": Capturing Children's Spirituality through Photography

Angela Veale, who introduced us to social mapping, briefly touches on another creative method for eliciting information about children's experiences. While she doesn't go into detail about how photography can be used to better understand children, she says that photography is a creative methodology, a type of participatory research that combines "scientific rigor and critical analysis with imagination and creativity as a means of coming to an interpretation of people's worlds within their cultural frames."[41] In other words, photography allows children to become active participants in the research process. It gives them freedom, ownership, creativity, and a "powerful new language"[42] to express their spiritual lives.

At the end of the second interviews, I gave a disposable camera with twenty-five exposures to each child and asked them to photograph the places and objects that help them feel close to and experience God or where and with which they feel safe, comfortable, or at peace. For legal reasons, I didn't ask them to take photos of people. The paperwork required for this would have given me a six-month-long headache. Nevertheless, some of the young photographers took pictures of the people in their lives anyway.

Over the next few weeks, the children captured images and brought back their cameras during the third focus groups. I had the photos developed before the fourth meetings (it was the first time I had film developed in a few years), and we spent most of these sessions discussing and looking at the photos. The photographers shared and described each of their pictures, told us why they took them, and said a little bit about how and why the place or object in the photo helps them to feel close to God, experience God, or feel safe. Like the process of drawing, having the children revisit their photos and explain why they captured each image worked together with the photos to create a more complete representation of the children's experiences and spirituality.

Although relatively few researchers have elicited information from children through photography,[43] this exercise proved to be a valuable

41. Veale, "Creative Methodologies," 254.

42. Clark, "Mosaic Approach," 145.

43. M. Brinton Lykes has used photography to research the experiences of women in postwar Guatemala (see Lykes, "Creative Arts") and Alison Clark made use of this method to study children in Britain (see Clark, "Mosaic Approach"). I am not aware,

means of understanding their inner lives. Each camera became a lens (pun intended) through which I could observe their spiritual lives. And by giving them cameras, I demonstrated that their experiences, ideas, and thoughts were important. The simple act of handing each child a camera with his or her name on it continued to build my rapport with the children and allowed all of the participants to know that they mattered.

Can I Get a Witness? Interviews with Parents

Another method of gathering information about children is to interview their parents or guardians. Although parents can't completely enter into their children's spiritual experiences, they can provide information that, when studied alongside other data, is useful in gaining a more complete blueprint of their children's spiritual experiences. In a sense, parents act as expert witnesses who see, hear, or know about their children's experiences and lives, thus qualifying them to testify their perceptions about such experiences.

After the children joined me for the third focus groups, I met with their parents in small groups. Although not all parents could attend these meetings, at least one parent of each child was present. Like the children's focus groups, these groups were arranged according to the churches involved in this study.

I began by explaining how these parents could help me gather information and I asked them to introduce themselves—even though most of them already knew one another. As with the focus groups with children, I told the parents what I was hoping to learn from them and how they could help me to better understand their children's spiritual experiences.

During these interviews, I asked parents questions about their views of spirituality, their involvement in their children's spiritual lives, and their perspectives of their children's spiritual experiences. In order to uphold confidentiality and protect the responses of parents from being skewed by predetermined information, I was cautious not to disclose any information that their children had provided during my discussions with them. I quickly learned, however, that the younger participants were often eager to chat with their parents about our conversations. Nevertheless, all of the parents were careful to provide me with their

however, of anyone who has used photography to research the spiritual experiences of children, other than Shelly Mecum (see Mecum, *God's Photo Album*).

perceptions of their children's spiritual lives and they certainly contributed a great deal to the research process.

In this chapter, I introduced you to the children and congregations involved in the research from which this book developed, as well as the methods that I used to explore their spiritual lives. Through these many forms of qualitative exploration—semi-structured focus groups with children, drawings, social mapping, photography, and interviews with parents—I was able to gain a window into the spiritual lives of the thirteen young pilgrims involved in this process. These methods allowed me to see many facets of the diamond.

These children, while not representative of all young people, graciously provided me with important information about spirituality, meaning making, and experiences with God and church. Their perceptions and ideas gave me a sense of the common journey that young people face as they walk along the spiritual path. What is more, these children became my guides, teaching me about faith, spirituality, and God. I am incredibly grateful to them for allowing me to enter into their spiritual experiences—their successes and disappointments, struggles and victories.

Children are spiritual makers of meaning who have much to offer those with ears to hear their voices. Yet too often, church leaders—and sometimes even parents—fail to truly listen to them. Perhaps it's because we assume that experts like Piaget and Spock (the famous pediatrician—not the character from *Star Trek*) can tell us more about children than the young people themselves. Perhaps we simply fool ourselves into believing we're too busy to take the time to hear children's voices. Perhaps, deep down, we are afraid that if we stop and really listen to the children in our lives, we may realize that we don't know them as well as we had thought. Whatever the reason, we need to realize that children matter and are worth the time and effort that is needed to understand them. "It seems only fair that, as teachers [or pastors or parents], we make an effort to see the world from the child's perspective."[44]

By examining the ways in which I explored the spiritual lives of these thirteen children, parents and practitioners can get a sense of how

44. Elkind, *Sympathetic Understanding*, 155.

they too might gain a window into the lives of the children in their care. While the methods I used can all be performed by pastors, teachers, and parents, they are certainly not one-size-fits-all. Some people may choose to carry out exploratory research in ways similar to what I presented in this chapter. Others might prefer to extract only those nuggets of information that are valuable to their specific situations. Still others may forge new ground by seeking their own ways to elicit information from the children in their midst. Whichever of these avenues one chooses, it's essential that adults who seek to nurture young people have ears to hear children's voices concerning their experiences, hopes, struggles, and ideas. When we do so, we can be better prepared to nurture their spiritual lives.

3

Four Ways of Knowing God

Explorations into the Spiritual Styles of Children

IN HER CLASSIC BOOK, *Natural Symbols*, Mary Douglas wrote that "the Sacred can be engraved in the hearts and minds of the worshippers in more ways than one."[1] After spending a considerable amount of time listening to the stories of my thirteen young friends, the truth of this statement became clear. Each child, as an active, spiritual, meaning-making agent, had his or her own ways of transcending, going beyond the here and now, and relating to God. For some, quiet times with their families played a key role in their personal and intimate times with God. Others met God while they were at Sunday school. Others sensed God's divine presence when they were alone in a quiet, secluded place among nature. Clearly, these children are capable of tapping into the spiritual and reaching out to God in ways that are all their own.

Yet amidst this diversity, four general approaches to spirituality— four *spiritual styles*—have been repeatedly manifested in the lives of these young people. In this chapter, I describe four spiritual styles, or broad ways through which people express their spiritual capacity, by sharing some of the information that the young focus group participants offered to me during my conversations and exercises with them. I'll examine commonalities and differences between the ways in which they express their inherent spirituality. This exploration is heavily influenced by the work of Urban T. Holmes, Corinne Ware, and Joyce Bellous, all of whom have written about different approaches to spirituality.

---

1. Douglas, *Natural Symbols*, xvii.

SPIRITUAL STYLES

Although these children exhibited different ways of expressing their spirituality, I was able to categorize them based on significant commonalities. Rather than reinventing the wheel, I examined the work of key scholars and practitioners to see if their ideas could capture the rich experiences of the children from Lawrence Park, Townsend, and Northview. After all, one can see farther while standing on the shoulders of giants. After a great deal of searching, I found that the writings of Bellous and Ware proved to offer a typology that best reflected the spiritual experiences of the thirteen children. Building on Holmes's theories, both of these authors present four personalities or types of spirituality: head, heart, mystic, and kingdom.

Since first conducting this research, I have collaborated with Joyce Bellous and Denise Peltomaki to recast these four broad categories of spirituality into what we refer to as *spiritual styles.* While Ware speaks of her spiritual types within the realm of Judeo-Christianity, we believe that spiritual styles extend beyond these religious traditions. They describe ways in which human beings actively express their inherent spirituality and ultimate concerns and they can capture the spiritual experiences of Christians, Jews, Muslims, Sikhs, and even atheists. Each spiritual style illustrates key aspects of the human quest to make meaning and connect with other people, the world, and God. We label these four styles *word, emotion, symbol,* and *action.*

Drawing from our research and experiences in leading prototype spiritual styles exercises, Bellous, Peltomaki, and I created two assessment tools that help people to discover their own dominant styles as well as understand the styles of those around them.[2] The first assessment tool is intended for adults and older youth and includes an introduction, forty assessment questions, reflection questions, and case studies. The second tool consists of questions and case studies for children and is meant to be led by adults who have already used the adult tool. Both assessment tools are available individually and in kits, which include an instructional DVD and all materials needed for conducting group assessments in congregations, schools, or retreats.[3]

2. Bellous et al., *Spiritual Styles.* Bellous et al., *Spiritual Styles—Children's Version.*
3. Spiritual styles assessments are available online at http://www.tallpinepress.com.

Each style speaks of spiritual experience generally, providing distinct yet fluid and porous boundaries in which people live out their innate spirituality. While most people possess one dominant spiritual style, characteristics of others often overlap and flow into one another. Furthermore, human beings are transforming creatures and our dominant styles can change throughout our lives. The dominant styles of the children I talked with may not characterize their spiritual lives as significantly ten years down the road as they did when I met with them.

This change has certainly been true for my life. As I look back at my experiences with church and with God, I can identify distinct times when my approach to spirituality was centered on words or emotion. At other times, my spiritual life was marked by symbols or actions. At still other times, no one style dominated the landscape of my spiritual life, but several worked together to color my experiences with God.

While most people have one or two styles that tend to dominate their spiritual experiences, a healthy spirituality possesses a degree of balance and maintains "a certain tension with those other dimensions that are not emphasized."[4] When such a balanced tension is absent, there is a dangerous tendency to fall into an aberration or extreme form of one style.

The concept of spiritual styles is a construction to aid in understanding different ways that people know and experience God. I do not offer it in an imperialistic fashion, demanding that all people fit into this fourfold framework for understanding spirituality. And I don't wish to be essentialist in my explanation, assuming that all people in all contexts express themselves through one or more of these four styles. These attitudes would counteract my purposes in writing this book: to demonstrate that there are multiple ways of expressing our spiritual lives and knowing God, that people require the freedom to connect with God in their own ways, and that ministries with children (and people of all ages) need to move beyond one-size-fits-all approaches. Spiritual styles is simply one idea for doing so.

What spiritual styles offer are partial, imperfect glimpses into people's inner lives. Since human beings can never be pinned down or wholly understood by typologies like spiritual styles, no one fits perfectly into any style and this fourfold typology cannot completely capture the spiritual capacities of all human beings. As we all color our lives, we will

4. Holmes, *History*, 5.

surely go outside of the lines and express ourselves in ways that are all our own. But I do believe that spiritual styles can assist people in making sense of their lives and the lives of others. They offer partial glimpses into the ways in which human beings make meaning and encounter the living God. We see through the glass dimly. But we do see through the glass (1 Cor 13:12).

Let me now outline each spiritual style, drawing from the work of scholars like Holmes, Bellous, and Ware. In addition to offering general information about the four styles, I'll "put feet" on the idea of spiritual styles by describing how they help us to make sense of the thirteen children who met with me for focus groups. In this way, I ground my discussion in the real lives of real children who express these four ways of knowing God and I make the whole concept of spiritual styles more accessible.

This chapter serves as an introduction to how spiritual styles are broadly understood. In the next chapter, I build on this discussion by describing the ways in which these styles were manifested in the lives of the thirteen children who were part of my research. It's important to remember that I'm describing broad categories. Even though each child possessed a dominant style, many combined different styles together in their spiritual lives and the ways they expressed these styles differed from child to child. Since the spiritual life is intimately personal at its core, each child will surely express and nurture this quality in unique and personal ways. No child perfectly fit within the mold of any one spiritual style (which is a good thing, for going too far into one style shuts out an openness to spiritual diversity and can lead to extremism of any style). With this in mind, let me paint a picture of each spiritual style using broad strokes.

The Spiritual Styles (and Ages) of Thirteen Children

	Word	Emotion	Symbol	Action
Northview Community Church	Ben (7)	Abigail (9)	Caleb (9)	
Townsend Baptist Church	Nicholas (9) Keira (10) Megan (9)	Owen (8)	Laurie (8)	
Lawrence Park Presbyterian Church		Houston (10) Gordon (8)	Freddy (10) Ian (7)	Juliet (10)

A Word-Centered Approach

For most of the twentieth century, western Christianity was dominated by a word-centered approach to spirituality. Even in the last few decades of the century, many publishers and teachers centered children's ministry around this spiritual style,[5] which is "a thoughtful, cognitive approach to spiritual experience based on the significance of words."[6]

People of this style focus on their intellectual thinking of God through what they can touch, see, and imagine. Their ability to engage in logical and rational thinking is their primary means for connecting with God and understanding the world.[7] By critically reflecting on God, they come to know God more. Words matter. And having the correct words in the correct order is important to people of this style. What is more, words do not only need to be in right relationship to one another—they also need to be in proper relationship with the concrete reality that they represent. Scripture, as the divine Word of God, is highly valued. God is often represented through anthropomorphic terminology, through language about human beings.

Since words are highly important, reading is seen as a key means through which God communicates[8] and the spoken word is important in religious services, often taking the form of Scripture readings, sermons, devotions, and lessons. People of this style value precision, clarity,

5. Richards, *Theology*, 59.
6. Bellous and Sheffield, *Conversations*, 104.
7. Ware, *Discover*, 37. O'Brien, "4 Ways," 18.
8. Ware, *Discover*, 86.

and thoughtfulness in their use of words. Overall, the trans/formational goal of this style is to have one's cognitive understanding trans/formed and to make sense of, experience, and name that which is holy.[9]

This emphasis on Scripture and the spoken word became acutely evident to me during a conversation with a friend who had a spirituality centered on words. In discussing a special chapel service that was going to consist solely of worship through music, she expressed her disappointment that preaching would be absent from this service. In her opinion—which was not unusual for people who take a word-centered approach to spirituality—Christian experience requires the Word of God, or Scripture, especially in a well-written sermon.

People whose spirituality is dominated by words often enjoy attending Bible studies or small groups that are led by individuals who are knowledgeable of the Scriptures. In this way, they increase in their intellectual knowledge of God, the church, and the Bible. These people can be found studying the Bible and they typically love to read theological books. Popular feel-good Christian literature might be seen as too wishy-washy and shallow for these people. Instead, they often like to dive deep and read books and articles that others may find too dry, dogmatic, or academic. In general, people of this style love to learn about God and the Bible, and through this learning about God, they come to know God in a personal way.

Although this style of spirituality offers much to the arenas of theology, education, scholarship, and critical examinations of texts,[10] its extreme form, or aberration, breeds rationalism. According to Ware, a word-centered approach taken to its extreme can lead to "an overintellectualization of one's spiritual life with a consequent loss of feeling, often perceived as dogmatic and *dry*."[11] By ignoring the experiential, emotional, and inexpressible qualities of spirituality, such people risk believing that having the correct words, ideas, or interpretations is all that matters. These extremists are often seen as dry head-trippers[12] who ostracize others by "relentlessly pointing out that everyone who does not agree with their view is incorrect."[13]

---

9. Bellous, *Educating Faith*, 66.

10. Ware, *Discover*, 37–38.

11. Ibid., 38.

12. Ibid., 86.

13. Bellous, *Educating Faith*, 66.

Four of the children who met with me for focus groups expressed a word-centered approach to spirituality. These children—most of whom attended Townsend Church—were Nicholas, Keira, Megan and Ben. While they all held unique beliefs, made meaning in unique ways, and had unique experiences of God, the style that these four young people most clearly and frequently exhibited was a word-centered approach. Let me illustrate this style by describing my conversations with these children.

Throughout the focus groups, Nicholas made it clear that learning and having knowledge about God were at the core of his spiritual experiences. During one of our conversations, he told me that he felt close to God at Sunday school and at his church because, "I learn more about him . . . because it's all about God." When I asked him what he thought was important about Townsend's church building, he replied, "you learn about God here." Another time, he expressed his belief that the only thing that made the building of Townsend a church (as opposed to a community center, school, etc.) was that the people inside talk about God. When his artistic side came out, he drew a picture of his father because he read the Bible to Nicholas, which helped him to feel safe and close to God. He also spoke highly of his Sunday school teachers and pastor, because they "tell you about God and stuff that you want to learn about it." From early in my conversations with Nicholas, it became quite clear that he valued gains in his cognitive understanding of God through reading the Bible and through formal church instruction. All this verified that his spirituality was dominated by a word-centered approach.

Keira was a young lady who could talk your ear off. From the moment we met, she didn't hesitate to tell me all about her life—and she did so with great attention to detail. At first, it was difficult for me to pick up on her dominant spiritual style. It wasn't until mid-way through the research process, when she drew a picture of me because I helped her feel close to God, that I discovered her word-centered approach to spirituality—and life in general. While I was flattered by her drawing, I was curious about why she drew me instead of her parents, sister, or pastors. In her words, I helped her to know and feel close to God "because we're here talking about God." Clearly, speaking about God was important to her and helped to nurture her spiritual life. I was amazed that I didn't pick up on Keira's focus on words earlier, since every time I met her, she talked to me about the details of her life, carefully choosing the ways in which she described her experiences. After all, the right words in the right order mattered to her.

As Keira shared her photos, her word-centered approach was also clearly expressed. She had taken a photo of her house to show me where she felt close to God. She explained the photo by saying, "I've learned about God in that house. I've read the Bible [there]." Reading the Bible was an important practice for her because, "When I'm reading the Bible I learn about God and learning about God is good. . . . When you learn more about him it makes you smarter in the eyes of God." Intellectual capabilities seemed to be an avenue of God's grace and presence in her life. When she spoke about the people who helped her to know or experience God, she made the following comment about a favorite Sunday school teacher: "She explained everything very well so she never had to go over it any time . . . and she helped us learn about God." Keira's mother was also one of her key spiritual guides because she "refers to Bible verses." All of this goes to show that her dominant style was a word-centered approach.

Although Megan expressed a degree of emotion in her spirituality, she took a word-centered approach to her spiritual life. At one point in our conversations, she told me about a weekly house church group that her parents hosted in their home. Megan loved finding a spot on the living room floor in earshot of her parents and their friends, listening to them study the Bible and talk about matters of spirituality, religion, and faith. This spiritual eavesdropping helped her feel close to God because, "they're talking about God and it's fun to listen to what they talk about." Megan recently began attending a private Christian school and she had only good things to say about her teacher, Mr. Lane. He was a strong spiritual influence on her because "he helps me know God more because he teaches me about God in Bible [class]."

Megan's parents made comments that demonstrated that her spirituality was dominated by words. They spoke of the few times that she joined them in Townsend's worship services, saying, "She's paying attention to some of what's going on. . . . She'll sit there quietly. She won't doodle. She'll listen." The fact that she focused intently on the spoken word preached by her pastor goes to show the spiritual power that words had in Megan's life. Her parents also told me about the difference they had seen in her life since transferring her from public school to a private Christian school. Since changing schools, her intellectual and verbal reasoning about God had been "ratcheted up a few notches. . . . Now she's willing to discuss what her opinion is in terms of God and Bible verses and what not." The people and places in her life that helped her to know God and experience God in real and trans/forming ways were the people and places that helped her to know about God. Through knowing about God, Megan knew God.

From day one, Ben made me laugh. He had a silly way of bouncing into the room and he always had a joke or two to tell during our focus groups. He was a humorous, extroverted, and easy-going boy, which made it a little more difficult to pick out key qualities of any spiritual style that might mark his experiences. But after reading and reread-ing transcripts from our focus groups and examining his social maps, photos, and drawings, I began to notice that a word-centered approach emerged.[14] For example, he identified cognitive learning as one of the most important characteristics of the adult worship services and chil-dren's programs.

Through discussions and artwork, Ben told me that there were two people who really helped him feel close to God—his mother and me. According to him, we both spoke about spirituality through questions and discussions. He also told me that he experienced God in real ways in the office space where we met for focus groups. Evidently, our conversa-tions about God, faith, and his spiritual experiences had nurtured him and met his spiritual needs. The words we shared with one another mattered to him a great deal. Comments made by Ben's mother also confirmed that he expressed this spiritual style: "[Ben's] more likely intellectually to say something he learned, maybe more so than he'd talk about feeling stuff." Although it was difficult to discover his dominant style, Ben most clearly and frequently exhibited qualities of a word-centered approach to spirituality. No wonder he loved to tell jokes—he could make people laugh by putting the right words together in the right way!

An Emotion-Centered Approach

While the previous style is based on the importance of words, an emo-tion-centered approach to spirituality places one's feelings at the core of

---

14 Less often, I caught glimpses of an emotion-centered style within Ben's spiritual-ity. He made comments about how he enjoyed the music in the adult service and the "feelings" it gave him.

spiritual experiences. In Ware's words, "it is all heart—combined with the concrete, real-life stuff."[15]

While concrete representations of God are encouraged, people of this style place a high value on music, drama, dance, and personal testimonies pointing to God's interventions in one's life. Music is particularly important to people of this style, confirming what many music therapists have discovered: "There is an integral link between music and spirituality that dates back to the beginning of history. . . . Music is a natural human expression of emotion."[16] Speaking of his gifts of music and dance, the late Michael Jackson once said to Oprah Winfrey: "I believe that all art has as its ultimate goal the union between the material and the spiritual, the human and the divine. I believe that to be the reason for the very existence of art."[17] These are the words of a person whose spiritual life is based on emotion.

For people of this style, freedom of creativity, expression, and emotion is prized and God is seen as here and now, a present reality. And a personal relationship with this here-and-now God is a spiritual essential.[18] While people who focus on emotion are suspicious of intellectualism and academia, they're likely to emphasize evangelism through sharing personal experiences and direct communication with God.[19] This may seem like a focus on words and learning, but the words are used for another purpose—they're meant to evoke emotional responses. The trans/formational goal of this style is "personal renewal and this [style] offers the Christian community a clear witness of Christianity's message and power."[20]

The aberration of an emotion-centered approach to spirituality is pietism, the result of which is an "us versus the world" mentality and an increasing isolation from the world.[21] Extremists tend to place all people

15. Ware, *Discover*, 39.

16. Wlodarczyk, "Effect of Music Therapy," 154. In recent years, music therapists have addressed issues of music and spirituality. Some, such as Magill, believe that spirituality is at the core of music therapy, demonstrating the important transcendental role of music, especially for those of this spiritual style. See Magill, "Music Therapy," 1.

17. Michael Jackson, Interview with Oprah Winfrey, February 10, 1993.

18. O'Brien, "4 Ways," 21.

19. Bellous, *Educating Faith*, 67.

20. Ibid.

21. Ware, *Discover*, 40.

in a spiritual box in which all must have similar, emotionally-charged experiences.[22] Other aberrations include enthusiasm and emotionalism, which fail to scrutinize emotional responses to spirituality or acknowledge and deal with unresolved suffering, loss, or pain.[23] All that matters is feeling good in the moment. Extreme forms of this style can be contagious, as attested by Joel Osteen's feel-good sermons preached to over 40,000 weekly attendees. But these aberrations can lead to unchecked and chaotic leadership that disenchants followers through causes that are laden with emotion yet are worthless in the long run.[24]

This spiritual style seems to have dominated much of North American Christianity—especially evangelicalism—for the past few decades. This is a trend that Ware noticed in the 1990s: "Americans are shifting their allegiances from speculative religion, which is often seen to be dry, mainline intellectualism, to the affective, or the 'religion with heart.'"[25]

Perhaps in response to the dominance of a word-centered approach, our present culture is thirsty for experiences that involve high levels of emotion. It's not surprising that churches emphasizing this spiritual style often experience rapid growth.[26] Take, for example, the many megachurches that have grown quite quickly over the past two or three decades, most of which can be classified in this style: Willow Creek Community Church and Saddleback Church in the United States and (perhaps the most famous of all emotion-centered megachurches) Hillsong Church in Australia. The focus on musical, heartfelt worship in many congregations and the big business of the Christian music industry demonstrate the trend of churches to emphasize this spiritual style and individuals to hunger for emotional transcendence.

Four of my thirteen young conversation partners had spiritual lives that were significantly marked by emotion: Abigail, Owen, Houston, and Gordon. Abigail, from Northview Community Church, particularly expressed an emotion-centered style through her drawings and photos. When I asked her to draw a picture of a place at her church where she experienced God, she drew the room where she attended a large-group

22. Ware, *Discover*, 88.

23. Bellous, *Educating Faith*, 67.

24. Ibid.

25. Ware, *Discover*, 113.

26. Ibid., 87–88.

children's church program. This place mattered, she said with a twinkle in her eye, "because we do songs there." These songs aided her in knowing and experiencing God and they were her favorite aspect of her church's Sunday morning programs. In her depiction of this room, she meticulously drew the aspects relating to music (a guitar, a keyboard, and a screen on which lyrics are projected) and left out anything to do with lessons. She didn't even draw people playing these instruments! Her leaders and fellow children did not help her to know God as much as the musical instruments they played. As she took on the role of photographer, she captured images of some audio cassettes containing lyrical and instrumental worship songs "that they play [at Northview] and I feel close to God." Music was a conduit through which Abigail became caught up in the presence of the living God because it tapped into her emotions and touched her innermost being.

Owen was the only child from Townsend Baptist Church who strongly expressed an emotion-centered style of spirituality. As with Abigail, music played a key role in Owen's spiritual life. During the social mapping exercise, he took a long, hard look at the map of his church building, placed his finger on the sanctuary, and declared that it was a very important place in the church. It was in the sanctuary that the congregation gathered to "sing songs about God," and this was why this young boy believed it to be an important place. Owen loved to join the community in lifting up their voices through song. Although he didn't spend much time in Townsend's sanctuary, when he did join the rest of the congregation in musical worship, he experienced God in unique and meaningful ways. When it came to what made this building a church rather than a school or community center, Owen was certain that it had to do with the worship and singing that took place within its walls. Furthermore, when I asked Owen to draw a picture of someone who helped him to feel close to God or know God, he grabbed a pencil and created a sketch of his church's worship band. As with Abigail, Owen connected with God in a personal way through his emotions. Music reached to the core of his spiritual life because of its power to evoke strong emotional connections with the transcendent God.

Houston was one of two children from Lawrence Park Presbyterian Church whose spiritual lives were dominated by emotion. This became evident very early in our conversations. Throughout the focus groups, Houston told several stories about his involvement in music, drama, and the arts, all of which helped him to have emotionally-rich encounters with God. His cherished memories at his church included Christmas pageants, choir performances, and other artistic events that stirred his emotion. Clearly, Houston loved the spotlight. But it wasn't fame or recognition that led him to the stage time and time again; it was the awesome transcendental power of music and the dramatic arts. At one point he told me that he would have liked the children's choir to practice in the choir room (where the adults rehearse) and present a number of plays to the church. Singing had the power to capture his emotions and help him feel close to God, so he wanted to spend time in places specifically designated for music.

While Houston experienced God through music and drama in general, the place where God was especially close to him was the sanctuary, where he joined in with a mighty chorus of witnesses who sang their lives together in this special place. In his words, "God feels close to me when I sing into the sanctuary." If speaking with Houston wasn't enough to determine his spiritual style, his mother also told me about his love of music and drama, further confirming his emotion-centered spirituality.

I had some difficulty pinpointing the spiritual style that had the greatest impact on Gordon's life because he was fairly quiet and at times seemed to copy the words and actions of his older brother. This made it tricky to discern what he actually thought, felt, and experienced. After some time and analysis, however, I was able to confidently surmise that Gordon most often expressed an emotion-centered approach to spirituality. He had wonderful things to say about his church (the building and community of people) because of how it made him *feel*, the positive and spiritually-enriching emotions that it evoked. While looking at his photographs, Gordon told me that his guitar was really important to him because he loves music.

In addition, the affective, emotional nature of his spirituality surfaced when he began talking about how he likes "the old days. . . . My mom tells stories [about] when she was a kid and they sound all awesome." These stories gave him warm feelings and helped him to transcend ordinary reality and be spiritually transported to a different time and place, perhaps one in which he could more readily sense God's presence. While Gordon had a more balanced spiritual life than some of my other conversation partners, he tended to feel particularly close to God during moments of heightened emotion.

A Symbol-Centered Approach

At its core, a spirituality centered on symbols is mystical in the way it values symbols and their abilities to connect people with the transcendent.[27] People of this style put significant worth on the power of quiet and silence, listening and hearing, and "connecting with [and] spending time with God so as to enjoy union with God."[28]

While symbol-centered people speak with God through various forms of prayer, some avoid verbally talking about God, for words fall short of describing that which is transcendent as well as personal spiritual experiences. Any attempt to fully explain God is believed to lose that which is precious about God. People with a symbol-centered approach to spirituality are likely to agree with the words of popular author and pastor Rob Bell: "The Christian faith is mysterious to the core. It is about things and beings that ultimately can't be put into words. Language fails. And if we do definitively put God into words, we have at that very moment made God something God is not."[29]

Mystics can be passive, quiet, calm, and they often sit in silence waiting on God's presence to descend on them. They see God as a mystery—"more felt than spoken"[30]—and they tend to refer to God in non-concrete ways. People of this style emphasize the beauty of God, creation, ritual, and visual art for their symbolic powers to speak of the divine. They value prayer and they tend to "push the frontiers of spirituality, enabling us to imagine what we might do if we would be open enough."[31] The goal of this style is trans/formation that enables union with God.[32] Although this goal is ultimately unattainable, mystics are satisfied with the journey to discover this union.[33] An excerpt from the opening words of Peter Rollins's *How (not) to Speak of God*—a book infused with a symbol-centered approach to spirituality—echoes the valuing of process over product that is common for people of this style: "*being* a Christian always involves *becoming* a Christian."[34]

27. Bellous and Csinos, "Spiritual Styles," 217.

28. Bellous, *Educating Faith*, 64.

29. Bell, *Velvet Elvis*, 32.

30. Bellous, *Educating Faith*, 67.

31. Ware, *Discover*, 42.

32. Bellous, *Educating Faith*, 68.

33. Ware, *Discover*, 41.

34. Rollins, *How (not) to Speak*, 5–6.

Of the four spiritual styles, people with a symbol-centered approach are most likely to become uncomfortable and they often struggle to fit in with organized religion.[35] This was quite evident during a particular time that a colleague led a class at McMaster Divinity College through spiritual styles. After everyone in the class assessed their dominant spiritual styles, the leader asked if anyone felt as though they didn't fit within their congregations. After hands were raised, and eyes glanced around the room, my colleague discovered that the majority the people who felt out of place at their churches had a symbol-centered approach to their spiritual lives.

Quietism, the aberration of this spiritual style, leads to extreme passivity and withdrawal from reality and the world, thus robbing others of the gifts that mysticism offers to people of other styles. Those who practice aberrations of this style likewise experience a deficiency of the other three styles.[36] Examples of extreme symbol-centered individuals include several saints who practiced asceticism, including St. Anthony of the Desert and St. Francis of Assisi. Mystics must be careful not to deprive others of their spiritual style, for "without this mystical warmth to deepen and broaden spiritual experience, we are left with cold, hard ideas that cannot sustain us in the crises of life and do not explain the strange, supernatural encounters people have with spiritual realities, and with God, even when they say they are atheists."[37]

Of the thirteen children that met with me for the focus groups, three clearly possessed a symbol-centered spirituality, while another had significant tendencies of this style. Of the former three, one came from each congregation: from Northview Community Church, Caleb; from Townsend Baptist Church, Laurie; from Lawrence Park Presbyterian Church, Ian. Freddy, also from Lawrence Park, expressed himself in ways that allowed me to categorize him under this umbrella, even though he demonstrated a fair degree of balance between the other styles. Freddy was the child who seemed to have a spiritual life that had the most balance between the four styles. But he did lean toward a symbol-centered approach.

During my second focus group with Caleb, he began to tell me about places where he felt safe or where he was able to have encounters with

35. Ware, *Discover*, 41.

36. Ibid., 42.

37. Bellous, *Educating Faith*, 68.

God. He told me about a "fort" near his home where he enjoyed spending time. This fort, located among the tall grass on the peninsula of a small lake, gave Caleb a sense of peace. Another place where he found tranquil solace was a natural pond beside Northview's property,[38] where he liked to sit and watch Canada geese. In describing why he liked these places, he said, "Usually I don't feel peaceful—I feel overworked . . . I find that [at this pond]—I just don't know why—I just walk in there and I don't feel like I have to fear anything at all." These special spots allowed Caleb to experience a transcendental peace that surpasses understanding. Even though Northview had built a large in-ground pond and fountain in front of its building, Caleb was drawn to the natural beauty of the pond on the edge of the congregation's property.

Caleb was a lover of all things mysterious and his favorite subjects were ancient Egypt, Stonehenge, and the Bermuda Triangle—places shrouded in mystery and the unknown. He believed that the Bible and God are mysterious at their cores and he knew that many of these mysteries will not be solved for many, many years—if they are ever solved at all. According to him, his Sunday school teachers focused on what is known about God and rarely, if ever, wondered about the mysterious aspects of God. This frustrated Caleb because he felt as though "they're explaining the wrong things. . . . I feel like they're saying that there are no mysteries of him . . . when I know there are." In order to satisfy his spiritual needs, Caleb read the Bible to reflect on the mysterious, unknown qualities of God, followed by quiet time in his bedroom where he wondered about such things. Sometimes he would ponder for hours at a time.

Like Caleb, Laurie clearly and frequently demonstrated her symbol-centered approach to spirituality during the focus group conversations. She felt closest to God at a specific spot along the river across from her house, where she would lose herself in the awesome presence of God. "I sit by the river and I feel close to him . . . because I feel really peaceful with him. I feel really peaceful there and when it's peaceful it reminds me more of God than of things around me. . . . Most of the time I just sit [at this spot] alone." When she showed me a photo of this place, she said, "It also makes me feel close to God because I think about all the creations that could be in the water." When it came to the Bible, Laurie enjoyed

---

38. The pond of which Caleb spoke is not the artificial pond that was constructed at the front of Northview, but a small natural pond to the side of the church property.

hearing about stories of miracles because they were "really amazing and they're exciting."

Laurie's style of prayer, which she believed to be central to her spiritual life, further led me to believe that she had a symbol-centered approach. In her words, "God's listening to me and I feel like he's protecting [me from] all the dangers around me because I'm talking to him and he doesn't want me to get distracted. . . . He's just listening to me and that just makes me feel close to him." Although Laurie had trouble speaking about her most spiritual moments (a typical characteristic of this style), she clearly displayed the mystical side of her life.

Her mother verified my hypothesis about her spiritual style by telling me that "Laurie just seems to draw [spirituality] from everywhere." "Laurie loves it down by the river. She likes being outside. She's kind of a nature nut. And she also likes to read so she likes a quiet spot." Although she attended a conversional congregation, Laurie was certain that she was a Christian before she accepted Jesus by "welcoming him into her heart." She could just sense God's presence in her life. All of this goes to show that her spiritual life was dominated by a symbol-centered approach, one that pushed the boundaries of what many others believe to be central to Christian faith. She might say, along with Rob Bell, that "everything is spiritual."[39]

At first, I wasn't able to determine the spiritual style of Ian, the youngest child from Lawrence Park involved in the focus groups. Ian suffered from attention-deficit hyperactivity disorder (ADHD), which caused him to be restless and inattentive much of the time. So, instead of attending Sunday school, he accompanied Lawrence Park's director of Christian education as she made her rounds to all the classes.

After talking with him for some time and interviewing his mother, I surmised that Ian expressed an approach to spirituality centered on symbols. This fascinated me, for the calmness and stillness associated with this style seemed to be the polar opposite of what one would expect from a child with ADHD. But according to him, the places and times in which he felt closest to God involved quiet, solitude, and stillness. One such place was "in bed when I say prayers at night. It feels like God is close to me when I'm saying prayers and that's my space where I feel God the most." Ian's mother spoke about his love of nature, which is common for mystics: "He loves to be outside. He loves going for hikes."

39. Bell, *Everything is Spiritual.*

When asked to take photos of places where he felt close to God, he took a picture of the moon, because "I like the moon." In a true symbol-centered approach, Ian expressed his love of nature and its transcendental power to connect him with the God of creation without putting his experiences into too many words.

Freddy seemed to exhibit some key qualities of a symbol-centered spirituality, but his spiritual life was not dominated by this style to the same degree as Caleb, Ian, and Laurie. Like Ian, Freddy felt particularly close to God in his bed: "I pray on my bed and it reminds me of God." He took photographs of his bed, some natural places (a field, a waterfall), and several pieces of art that spoke of God (vines, flowers, animals, and quite a number of angels). Although he made comments demonstrating other styles, the symbolic and mystical aspects of his spirituality seemed to be most important to him. Perhaps his spiritual life was more balanced than many of the other children, even though he seemed to lean toward a symbol-centered approach.

An Action-Centered Approach

The final spiritual style has usually been the least common to be expressed within dominant Christian cultures in recent years, so it can be somewhat difficult to depict. But there seems to be a growing number of people, often within the missional church movement and other new forms of church, who express this spiritual style.

Similar to its symbol-centered neighbor, an action-centered approach affirms that God and the spiritual life cannot be fully expressed to others. However, these people believe that they need to do more than just pray for the world—they must actively and radically seek to transform it.[40] "This is the pathway of faith in action."[41] It involves giving of oneself in order to improve the world. People of this style strive to follow God's divine will and to assertively (and sometimes aggressively) help bring forth the coming reign of God. This can cause them to empty themselves, to "sacrifice their personal lives for their hope that the kingdom will be realized on earth."[42] In the tradition of the Lord's Prayer,

---

40. Bellous, *Educating Faith*, 68.

41. O'Brien, "4 Ways," 21.

42. Ware, *Discover*, 43.

these people use their actions to say to God, "your kingdom come, your will be done on earth as it is in heaven" (Matt 6:10).

Maintaining the tradition of the prophets, reformers, and liberation theologians, the trans/formational goal of this style is to change the oppressive, harmful, and destructive features of society while stressing the presence and justice of God.[43]

The action involved in this style shouldn't be confused with views of kinesthetic learning—that is, learning that comes through movement. While each style involves some types of action or movement—whether exploring libraries, dancing, or walking along a river—this fourth style involves a specific kind of action. People who express this style are particularly focused on action that seeks to make the world a better place, to transform the world into a place of justice, equality, and care for all people and for the earth. The actions of this style are about ripping out the roots of injustice in the world and planting seeds of compassion, love, and justice. Although they can evoke embarrassment or anger in others for pinpointing the unjust aspects of their lives, these people aren't usually too concerned with how they are viewed or judged. They are rather impulsive and avoid the restraint of regulations and rules.[44] Hence, they care less about organizational or denominational affiliations than do other individuals.[45]

The distorted or unbalanced form of an action-centered approach to spirituality is encratism, which consists of a single-minded "tunnel-vision" in which those who do not espouse unbridled support for a cause are seen as outsiders.[46] Since action is so fundamental to this style, encratists see little use for words and are often inarticulate about their goals and theological assumptions. This can make it quite difficult to rally others together in support of their causes.[47]

Only one child out of the thirteen demonstrated a tendency toward this style, perhaps affirming that this is the least common spiritual style. Juliet, the ten-year-old participant from Lawrence Park Presbyterian Church, spoke of her desire to help those in need from the beginning of our first meeting, when I asked all the children to tell me a story about one

43. Bellous, *Educating Faith*, 68.
44. O'Brien, "4 Ways," 22.
45. Ware, *Discover*, 43.
46. Ibid., 44.
47. Bellous, *Educating Faith*, 69.

of their best memories at their congregation. Eager to begin, Juliet told me that she loved helping with events that her church ran for the home- less in their downtown area, specifically a free barbeque that Lawrence Park had hosted a few months earlier. She loved "the fact that I'm helping the homeless. And it's really fun doing it at the same time." Participating in such events aimed at aiding the poor of the downtown area gave Juliet a sense of self-worth and fulfillment and helped her to experience the presence of God. Since she worked alongside members of her faith com- munity of many different age groups, her participation in these events allowed her to feel like a legitimate member of the congregation.

After receiving her disposable camera and instructions to photo- graph places and things that made her feel close to God, Juliet snapped only six shots out of a possible twenty-five. But each of these few pho- tographs was intentionally taken in because it captured the things that mattered most to her spiritual life. Two of the photos depicted her Operation Christmas Child (OCC) shoe box. OCC is a campaign run by Samaritan's Purse that encourages people of all ages to bring "joy and hope to children in desperate situations around the world through gift- filled shoe boxes and the Good News of God's love."[48] By filling a shoe box with toys, books, and clothes for a child in an impoverished country, Juliet had a profound spiritual experience—one so important to her that she took two photos in order to ensure that the box was clearly visible. In her words, OCC is "when you give a box of gifts to a child in another country. And it helps me feel close to God because I'm giving to other people." Juliet related helping those in need with experiencing God, a common characteristic of this spiritual style. While her Bible, as depicted in another photo, provided her with the written word that grounded her practical theology, her beliefs were not complete until she put them into action through helping others obtain justice.

During my interview with the parents of the children from Lawrence Park, Juliet's mother made comments that confirmed my belief that her daughter's spirituality was dominated by action. After sharing her view of spirituality, she told me that she thought Juliet was becoming more mature in her faith because, "She's starting to realize that what she learns [at church] needs to have some sort of impact in what she does. And I sit with her and listen to her prayers at night and . . . it's changed a little bit

---

48. Samaritan's Purse, "Uplifting the Outcasts."

from, you know, 'Thank you for a mommy who loves me so very much'
... to 'Help me to make a difference in the world.'"

She went on to say that Juliet had been reading books about social
action and social responsibility by Craig and Marc Kielburger, founder
and CEO of Free the Children, a Toronto-based organization that fights
child labor and other injustices and advocates for the education of children living in poverty.[49] These books had inspired her to begin raising
money to build a school in an impoverished nation through Free the
Children's Brick-by-Brick Campaign,[50] a project that she had wanted to
undertake for some time.

While her mother was excited about the fruits of Juliet's spirituality, she wanted to keep Juliet's goals realistic and support her "without
putting up too many roadblocks." She was quite aware that her daughter's spirituality was centered on action, for she ended her discussion of
Juliet's desire to help others with a short, profound statement: "That's her
spirituality."

Spiritual styles help to make sense of the spiritual lives and experiences
of children. In this chapter, I have outlined the four spiritual styles—
word, emotion, symbol, and action—in order to initiate a discussion
about what exactly spiritual styles are, why they matter, and how children make use of them in making meaning and expressing the spiritual
dimension of their lives. As the children in these pages have shown us,
there are countless ways in which young disciples express and make
meaning through these four broad approaches to spirituality.

While there are certainly characteristics that are unique to each
spiritual style, there is a degree of overlap between different styles. For
example, planting trees or picking up litter at a conservation area might
be important to a person with a spirituality focused on action or symbols. For the action-centered person, such practices are directly aimed

49. Craig Kielburger founded Free the Children to fight against child labor and
encourage education when he was twelve years old. Since its founding in 1995, Free
the Children has grown into "the world's largest network of children helping children
through education . . . [and has] changed the lives of more than one million children."
Kielburger and Kielburger, *Me to We*, 11.

50. For more information about this program, see http://www.freethechildren.com/
we/adoptavillage/bbb.htm.

at making the world a better place through caring for the planet and combating ecological degradation. For the symbol-centered person, the focus may be on ensuring that the wonder and beauty of the natural world is preserved. Another example might be writing songs to God. A person who emphasizes emotion might focus on how the melody, harmony, and lyrics are intricately woven together to foster emotional connections with God, while a word-centered person might pay particular attention to the lyrical content, ensuring that the lyrics reflect accurate and appropriate theological views for their context. Clearly, spiritual styles are distinct from one another but not mutually exclusive.

In the next chapter, I use the information that I gathered from the children to examine what is important to young people who express each spiritual style. I draw out common elements of each style in order to further explain how they affect children's spiritual lives, connections with God, and experiences at their faith communities. Then, in chapters 5, 6, and 7, I turn to strategies and tactics that are helpful for nurturing and including children of each style and for providing each young person with a sense of fit.

4

Beyond One-Size-Fits-All

Further Explorations into the Spiritual Styles of Children

A FEW YEARS AGO, Greg Hawkins, Executive Pastor of Willow Creek Community Church in Illinois, revealed the surprising results of a major study that his church undertook. Hawkins had begun questioning his church's ability to authentically reach people and assist them in experiencing Christian trans/formation. In 2004, he formed a research study to examine the spiritual lives of several of Willow Creek's congregants in order to determine if his church, which has a ministry that spans the globe, was really making a difference in the lives of its members. Afterwards, he took the study on the road and included thousands of people from other congregations in his research. The results shocked him and they have dramatic implications for the ways in which churches trans/form human lives.

The first surprising finding his study uncovered was that his fundamental presupposition for ministry was flawed. He had assumed that having greater numbers of people engage in greater amounts of church activities and programs would produce better disciples of Christ. His research found that those who participated in many church programs were actually stalled in their relationships with God and their spiritual growth, which he defined as "An increasing love for God and for other people,"[1] based on Jesus' words in Matthew 22:37–39. He discovered that those who were exceptionally committed to following Christ (people to whom he refers as "close to Christ" and "Christ-centered")[2] were becom-

1. Hawkins and Parkinson, *Reveal*, 29.
2. Ibid., 37.

ing increasingly dissatisfied with their church's programs and activities. In a short video in which he explains the primary results of this study, he says that people who are close to Christ and Christ-centered are "disappointed with the role the local church is playing in their lives. And increasingly these people are thinking about leaving the [institutional] church."[3]

Apparently increasing attendance and levels of participation within the life of a church does *not* predict that one is growing in one's love of God and people.[4] The implications of this turned the Willow Creek pastor's view of effective ministry on its head. Hawkins came to see that "The health of the church is not just about the numbers. When it comes to spiritual growth, we need to be able to measure the unseen. We need a glimpse of people's attitudes, thoughts, and feelings. We need words that reveal the heart of each person. We want to know what moves them at the deepest levels. We need to ask, 'Where are you?'"[5]

Through this book, I have set out to "measure the unseen," to explore how churches nurture children's spirituality and where young people are in their experiences with congregations and their encounters with God. My quest was focused on talking with thirteen children about their spiritual experiences—experiences that are not relegated solely to the activities and programs in the life of their congregations.

A second finding of the research that Hawkins and his church undertook was that at different stages in their spiritual growth, people have different spiritual needs. For example, he found that those who are new to the Christian faith, but are "growing in Christ," benefit from small groups and simple individual spiritual practices, while those who are "Christ-centered" require opportunities to authentically mentor and serve others, perhaps those who are new to the faith.[6] For some people, this finding is yesterday's news. But for others who hold different perspectives of ministry and spiritual trans/formation, this is a startling finding.

While I affirm Hawkins's assertion that people at different stages of spiritual trans/formation and growth require different approaches to ministry, I take it further by adding that people of different spiritual

3. Hawkins, "Watch Greg Hawkins."
4. Hawkins and Parkinson, *Reveal*, 13.
5. Willow Creek Association, "The REVEAL Story."
6. Hawkins and Parkinson, *Reveal*, 39.

styles also have different needs, as we began to see in chapter 3. Although people in the same church have very different spiritual needs, Hawkins found that most churches that he studied, including Willow Creek, present a "one-size-fits-all" ministry style.[7] This means that congregations provide ministries, programs, activities, and spiritual direction under the assumption that all people possess similar or identical spiritual needs.

This may have been the assumption under which Northview Community Church was operating, for Caleb's words about the church "explaining the wrong things"[8] demonstrate that its ministries and programs are not meeting his symbol-centered needs. But, as my research and the research of Willow Creek would agree, people have very different spiritual needs. Therefore, churches do well to heed the advice of Karen Tye, a Christian educator who believes that "we have to set aside our one-size-fits-all perspective in order to educate in ways that will engage people and help them grow."[9]

Let us do just that. As we dig deeper into our exploration of children's spiritual styles, let us forget, if even for a moment, about models of ministry that operate based on one-size-fits-all approaches to spiritual trans/formation and growth. Let us remove the limitations that we place on the human spirit and the Spirit of God. If we are to treat those children who offer us glimpses into their inner lives with dignity and respect, no less is required of us.

DIGGING DEEPER INTO SPIRITUAL STYLES

Object relations theory, as we discussed in the first chapter, presupposes that everyone makes meaning of people and places in unique ways. Based on a myriad of experiences, relationships, and many other factors, people make sense of the world around them differently. Amidst this diversity, people often express and understand their spirituality and faith traditions in four broad ways: through words, emotion, symbols, and action. But this does not imply that all people who possess the same spiritual styles have identical spiritual needs. Rather, within each style, human beings may make meaning differently than other people of the same style. Let me offer an example to clarify this assertion.

7. Hawkins, "Watch Greg Hawkins."

8. See page 63 in chapter 3.

9. Tye, *Basics*, 41.

Megan and Keira were two girls, ages nine and ten, who both attended Townsend Baptist Church and who both had a word-centered approach to spirituality. Despite these commonalities, however, when I asked them what they thought made their congregation's building a church, rather than a community center, a school, or another type of building, their opinions were radically different.

Keira thought the Christian people who spent time within the building had much to do with its existence as a church. Evidently, she wouldn't have thought of her church's building as a church if it had been filled with people attending an Avril Lavigne concert or a motivational speech by Tony Robbins. Megan, on the other hand, supposed that the outdoor sign that graces the entrance of the church's parking lot clearly made the building a church. After all, it did say Townsend Baptist *Church*. It is clear that these two individuals, who possessed significant biological, cultural, and spiritual similarities, made meaning of my question and the nature of their church's building in very different ways.

When interacting with children and providing them with spiritual direction, it's important for parents and ministry leaders to acknowledge the uniqueness of each person's ways of making meaning. Still, there are significant characteristics that are shared by people of the same spiritual style. These commonalities provide us with some conceptual clarity about what is involved with each style and, as we'll see in the next few chapters, they can aid pastors, parents, and teachers as they seek to help children engage in spiritual trans/formation.

Throughout the remainder of this chapter, I draw from the lives of the thirteen young people I have come to know in order to offer further insight into the four spiritual styles, especially as they are manifested in the lives and experiences of children. As you read this chapter, you may want to think about the young people you know and those involved in your ministries. How are they similar to or different from the lives of the children in the following pages? How can their experiences add to this conversation about children's spiritual styles?

Growing in Knowledge and Wisdom within a Word-Centered Approach

For children who express a word-centered style of spirituality, the Bible is of the utmost importance to their connections with God and is central to their spiritual lives. While texts and words in general are essential for people of this style, the Bible is seen as the Text above all texts and the Word above all words.

This point was made quite clear by Nicholas, Keira, and Megan, each of whom spoke of the vital importance of the Bible in their lives. However, Ben didn't clearly identify the Bible as central to his life. But he did speak very fondly of his VeggieTales DVDs, which he pinpointed as the only objects through which he experienced God.

Created by Phil Vischer, VeggieTales is a popular video series in which cartoon vegetables act out variations of traditional Bible stories, such as David and Goliath or Joshua and the fall of Jericho. At the end of each episode, the hosts, Bob the Tomato and Larry the Cucumber, apply the story featured in the episode to children's lives with the help of a Bible verse from their aptly-named computer, Qwerty. The importance that Ben placed on his collection of VeggieTales DVDs demonstrated that the Bible (or at least the stories within the Bible) was significant to his spiritual life. For these four children, the critical role of the Bible was clear when they said that one of the key ways that their parents helped them to know God was by reading the Bible or assisting them in learning Bible verses. Knowing God, for these children, was often equated with having knowledge about the Bible.

The three young word-centered people from Townsend (Nicholas, Megan, and Keira) often spoke of the important roles that their congregations played in their spiritual lives. For example, although Nicholas didn't mind spending time in his church's worship center (or sanctuary) he much preferred to be in the gymnasium or in his classroom, where he heard and studied the Bible. Megan and Nicholas both seemed to talk about their church in this capacity more frequently than did Ben and Keira. When I asked Nicholas to identify a specific place in his church where he felt close to God, he told me that this would have been difficult to do, for he experienced God throughout the entire church building. From these comments, it could be surmised that Townsend was adequately meeting the needs of children whose spiritual style was a word-centered approach.

Ben, the only child from Northview Church who had a word-centered spirituality, identified the room in which we met for focus groups as the place in his church where he was most apt to experience God. Although this place was in his church's building, it had nothing to do with Northview's children's ministries and Ben only occupied this space for our focus groups. Until he began meeting Abigail and me there for our conversations, he had never even been in this room! Ben spoke highly of this office and didn't even mention other spaces in his church where he experienced God. This led me to suspect that his congregation might not have been meeting Ben's spiritual needs, and perhaps those of other word-centered children. Ben's family members (and apparently I as well) took the primary role in nurturing his spiritual life by watching VeggieTales videos or talking with him about God.

Robert, the first earl of Lytton, who wrote poems under the name of Owen Meredith, once said, "It is, however, not to the museum, or the lecture-room, or the drawing-school, but to the library, that we must go for the completion of our humanity. It is books that bear from age to age the intellectual wealth of the world."[10] Church libraries and resource centers seemed to be particularly important to young people of this spiritual style. Many of the children who expressed a word-centered spirituality spoke very fondly of their church's libraries for their ability to help them connect with God. This is consistent with the nature of this spiritual style, for spoken and written words are of central importance to these people for their ability to offer knowledge about God. And libraries are storehouses of words about God, the Bible, and spirituality. By spending time browsing through the books and resources contained within church libraries, children open themselves not only to the "intellectual wealth of the world," but to the intellectual wealth of God.

With what we know of these children so far, it's not surprising to learn that they identified people who talk about God and teach them about the Bible, especially Sunday school teachers, as the individuals who helped them to experience God. For example, Keira told me about a Sunday school teacher who "explained everything very well so she never had to go over it any time. . . . She was very nice and she helps us learn about God." Megan discussed the vital role that Sunday school teachers have had in her life and drew a picture of one such teacher, Mr. Donaldson, holding items he used for lessons. She and her parents also spoke highly of her teacher at her private Christian school, Mr. Lane, for, in her father's words, "Megan's getting some very good, quality learning . . . through him." Nicholas learned a great deal about the Bible and God through his homeschool classes, led by his mother, and family devotions, led by his father, so he spoke of his parents as

10. Quoted in Alexander Ireland, *The Book-Lover's Enchiridion*, 430.

those who had a significant impact on his spiritual life. As I already mentioned, Ben identified his mother and me as those who helped him feel close to God, for we talked with him about God, and, in this way, we nurtured his spiritual style.

It is evident that children whose spirituality is dominated by words and by the illumination of the mind are most influenced by those who talk about God and help them to better understand the Bible. The spiritual needs of the children from Townsend Baptist Church were adequately met by their Sunday school teachers. For Ben, his mother and I—those outside of the church's children's ministries—were most important. While parents ought to be vital influences in the spiritual trans/ formation of their children, this further revealed that Northview might not have been completely inclusive of children who expressed a word-centered spiritual style. After all, Ben was the only word-centered child who didn't mention his congregation when talking about what nurtured his spiritual life.

Let me summarize some of the key spiritual needs of children of this style. Young people who have a word-centered approach to spirituality need to be surrounded and influenced by people who can adequately engage them in learning about God and the Bible through lessons, devotions, and personal conversation. They need people who profess truths about God through the spoken and written word. The Bible is central to their lives, and those who read and teach the Bible to these children profoundly impact their spirituality and can aid in their trans/formation. The places where they are apt to experience God include those where people speak of God and where the Bible is taught and books are read, especially Sunday school classrooms and church libraries. These four children readily demonstrate that "Scripture is highly valued. Words and accuracy are important. . . . The transformational goal is personal understanding."[11]

Feeling God's Presence within an Emotion-Centered Approach

As I mentioned in the previous chapter, music is at the core of an emotion-centered approach to spirituality. This proved to be true for the children involved in my research. The four young people whose spiritual lives were dominated by emotion (Houston, Gordon, Abigail, and

11. Bellous, *Educating Faith*, 66.

Owen) placed high value on affective experiences with music. Music had the transcendental ability to tap into their innate spirituality and allow them to experience God in unique and personal ways.

It is not surprising, therefore, that the places where these children heard and made music—especially religious music—were important to them. For Abigail, one key place was her children's church room, where she sang songs of worship with other young people. She appreciated the fact that Northview Community Church had a children's band that led children in musical worship. Worshipping with this band helped her to transcend ordinary space and time and sense the presence of the Almighty. For Owen, the sanctuary was important because the adults (and visiting children) sang worship songs there, a practice that nurtured his spirit.[12] Houston identified multiple spaces within Lawrence Park's building as those places where music fed his spirituality, including the choir room, the sanctuary, and the summer children's church room. Gordon also loved to be in the sanctuary, where he engaged in musical worship to God, and he was eager to say that he wanted to spend more time with his family in this place.

Like word-centered children, young people who focus on emotion identified their Bibles as important objects in their spiritual lives. Owen made this point quite evident when he told me that the Bible "helps me experience more about God." Abigail was sure to snap a photograph of her Bible to show to me because it helped her to know God. As with their word-centered neighbors, these children emphasized the role of the Bible in their spiritual life. For them, the Bible had the unique ability to help them know God in emotionally-intimate and personal ways. Rather than seeing the Bible as a storehouse of information about God, perhaps they might have been more apt to agree with Billy Graham that, "The Bible is God's 'love letter' to us, telling us not only that He loves us, but showing us what He has done to demonstrate His love."[13]

According to these children, congregational worship—which often stresses emotional responses through religious music—was a necessary component of the life of the church. When the children and I chatted about what they felt was important for visitors to know about their con-

12. It is interesting to note that Owen did not spend a significant amount of time in the regular services of his church, yet these rare moments were vital to his spiritual life.

13. Graham, "Bible is God's 'Love Letter.'"

gregation, most spoke of the activity of worship that took place within its walls. While Abigail explicitly answered by saying, "there's worship," Owen pointed to the worship center (or sanctuary) on a map of his church, saying that it was an important place "because they sing songs about God." During another interview, Owen ruminated on what it was that made Townsend's building a church, rather than a school. Although his word-centered brother thought what made it a church was the fact that the community inside the building talked about God, Owen disagreed, stating that, "there are Christian schools and maybe in Christian schools they talk about God." In the end, he decided that the worship center was what made the building a church, for through the worship that occurred in this space, people could have emotional connections to God. Evidently, acts of worship, which each of these churches associates with emotive responses to music, are vital to the life of children whose style of spirituality is emotion-centered.

Since the contemporary church in the west seems to be dominated by an emotion-centered approach, it's not surprising that all three congregations—Northview, Townsend, and Lawrence Park—emphasized and nurtured this spiritual style in their ministries and programs. Every child who shared this spiritual style expressed a deep fondness and appreciation for their congregation's ministries and leaders and the spiritual nourishment they received from them.

During the social mapping exercise, I gave my young conversation partners an opportunity to describe any changes they would like to make to the physical location of people within their congregations.[14] While most of the children altered their church's demographics in various ways, two children didn't change their social maps at all. Abigail and Owen, both of whom had an emotion-centered approach to spirituality, were completely satisfied with where children and adults resided during church services. While I was surprised that they wouldn't change a single thing about the location of people in their churches, it demonstrated that their congregations were meeting their spiritual needs through the structures and demographics of Sunday programs and services. After all, the ministries at their faith communities included elements geared toward those who shared this spiritual style.

All four children also spoke fondly of their church leaders as people who helped them to feel God's presence or with whom they experienced

14. See pages 41–42 in chapter 2.

God. Both children from the Presbyterian congregation told me that their church's minister nurtured their connection with God. Through a drawing, Houston also identified Lawrence Park's director of Christian education as a person who assisted him in knowing God. Abigail had fond things to say about past and present Sunday school teachers who fed her emotionally-rich spiritual style. Owen specified his church's worship band and his Sunday school teachers as those who helped him experience God, but expressed a general feeling that many people at his church influenced his spiritual life in positive ways. Since several of the leaders and ministers at these churches emphasized an emotion-centered style of spirituality through leading children in activities involving music, drama, and the arts at their respective ministries, it makes sense that the people at these congregations nurtured children of this style.

According to these four children, there are certain objects, places, and people that are important to those who have a spirituality dominated by one's feelings. The Bible, as a means by which God is revealed, is valued for its usefulness in knowing God in affective ways. Since music is such a vital component of the spiritual life of children of this style, the spaces in which congregations make music are important, and children enjoy spending time in these places. In addition, musical worship is an effective means for tapping into young people's spirituality and allowing them to feel the presence of God. Congregations that emphasize worship during their Sunday services and programs lead emotion-centered children to focus on this celebratory event as a vital characteristic of their churches and their first-hand encounters with God. The people who have the greatest impact on these young people are those who lead them through affective, emotional experiences with the transcendent God, like corporate worship and music.

Seeking the God of Mystery within a Symbol-Centered Approach

Gandhi once said, "In the attitude of silence the soul finds the path in a clearer light." This statement reflects the attitudes of the four children who had a symbol-centered style of spirituality—Caleb, Freddy, Laurie, and Ian. These young people valued quiet solitude as part of their spiritual experiences. While Freddy demonstrated a need for solitude and quiet through a picture of a field where he sat and listened to the leaves in the wind, Ian told me that he felt close to God in his bathroom and bedroom, places where he spent time in quiet solitude. As I mentioned in the last chapter, Caleb loved to sit beside a pond near his church as well as at a fort near the lake in his neighborhood. In both of these places, he felt a sense of peace and quiet that he didn't receive elsewhere, largely because he could spend some silent time by himself in these places. Laurie would walk down to the river where she loved to sit in quiet solitude, looking at the animals and water. In her words, "I feel really peaceful there and when it's peaceful it reminds me more of God." She also liked being on the beaches of Lake Huron, where she could quietly listen to the wind rustling through the leaves and the water lapping against the shoreline. Silence and solitude were important to these children, many of whom had "special spots" where they would spend quiet time and receive spiritual nourishment.[15] It was when these children were alone and quiet that they sensed God's presence around them.

An emphasis on prayer was another common characteristic of children with a symbol-centered spirituality, although each young person who expressed this style spoke of this practice in unique ways. Laurie showed that she valued prayer by taking a photo of her sister's hands folded in a typical prayer formation. Freddy used his camera to demonstrate the importance of prayer through a picture of an armchair in his house where he liked to sit and talk with God. Ian told me that his special place was "in my bed when I say prayers at night. It feels like God is close to me when I'm saying prayers and that's my space where I feel God the most." Caleb was the only child who didn't discuss his prayer life in detail. The other children, however, were quite open about their love of connecting with God through prayer. Prayer provided spiritual nourishment and helped them have spirit-to-Spirit connections with the Mystery of Mysteries.

As one may have noticed from what I have already said about these four children, the natural world was of great significance to their spiritual lives. Laurie made this very clear when we met for the last time. Toward the end of this meeting, I offered the children a final opportunity to tell me any other important or pertinent information about their spirituality, their spiritual experiences, or their relationship with God. Laurie made a point of expressing her love of the natural world: "I also like the animals, but just everywhere, in trees and stuff." She then seemed to, in her head,

15. Through his qualitative research, Tobin Hart also noticed that some children have special places that "provide a kind of spiritual nourishment." Hart, "Spiritual Experiences," 165.

run through a longer list of elements of nature that she loves. But instead of telling me every detail, she simply said, "So, basically, nature." From dirt and water to birds and the wind, this young woman soaked up the natural world in a way that nurtured her spirit and allowed her to sense the presence of the Creator. Her mother verified her love of nature by calling her a "nature nut."

This was a sentiment that Ian's mother also expressed regarding his preferences, which were confirmed through his words and photos, one of which captured the moon. When I asked Ian why he took a photo of the moon, he avoided putting his reason into words, a characteristic of a true mystic. Instead, he simply said, "I like the moon." As previously mentioned, Freddy liked to sit outside in a field near his home listening to the sounds of nature, the sounds of God. Caleb also loved nature, especially animals, so he enjoyed sitting at the water's edge and watching the wildlife as it swam, crawled, and flew among God's creation.

It was clear that each of the symbol-centered children spoke fondly of the role of nature in their spiritual lives, demonstrating that, as Dori Baker and Joyce Mercer have said, nature is "a special locus of divine revelation and a place for humans to encounter God."[16] The spiritual lives of these four children were nurtured through direct contact with God's natural creation. Putting images of oceans, forests, and mountains behind lyrics projected during worship services just couldn't tap into the spirits of these children. They needed to experience nature first-hand, to run, sit, climb, walk, and play among it. Engaging with nature seemed to be a form of prayer—through it, they had first-hand encounters with God.

Since these four children enjoyed spending time out of doors, it shouldn't be shocking to learn that most of them preferred to be in wide, open spaces. Unfortunately, three of these children informed me that they felt crowded at their churches. Spaces like Sunday school classrooms, which exist to nurture the spiritual life of children, often made these young people feel cramped, squished, and uncomfortable. Referring to different rooms at her church, Laurie exemplified this feeling by saying, "I like the big [rooms] because whenever I'm in the little ones I feel all shoved up—like I'm being crammed inside of a locker." Ian also identified his preference for open spaces by telling me that he wished the people at his church could spend more time outside.

16. Baker and Mercer, *Lives to Offer*, 55.

Although these children experienced God most readily during times of solitude, each of them also spoke of the importance of their families in their spiritual lives. Their parents, siblings, and extended family members might have played different roles in nurturing them, but these family members helped these children experience God and transcend the here and now.

Through their photographs and artwork, the children identified family members as the people with whom they sensed God's presence. While Caleb captured photographs of his parents and sister, he also drew a picture of his father. Through quality time together, they helped to nurture Caleb's spirit in ways that leaders and ministers at his church could not. The individuals who allowed Ian to connect with God included his mother, grandfather, and brother. Laurie photographed her mother, father, and two siblings and meticulously painted a picture of her parents to show how important they were to her spiritual life. Freddy's roll of film included a picture of his brother and his art portfolio contained a painting of key spiritual leaders in his life, including his parents. Although it was unusual for these children to spend long periods of time at church with their families, these were the people with whom the children are most apt to have real encounters with God and to have their spirits nurtured. These close familial relationships nurtured these young people in ways that relationships with Sunday school teachers and pastors could not.

In summary, children with a symbol-centered approach to spirituality tend to value places with plenty of room where they can quietly spend time alone with God. Since they love nature, these places are often outside. Some of them might feel crowded and uncomfortable in Sunday school classrooms and may prefer to explore and experience God's creation first-hand. Prayer is a vital practice for these children, which is often manifested in quiet, private, and personalized ways. Finally, the families of symbol-centered children tend to be key influences of their spiritual lives.

All of this shows that some of the churches involved in my research might not have been providing room for symbol-centered children in their ministries and programs. They do not seem to be places of inclusivity in which mystics feel a sense of fit and belonging. It was clear that, for the four mystics, connecting with God happened on a regular basis and wasn't confined to Sunday morning services and other church programs.

They experienced God during times of quiet solitude, in nature, through prayer, and with their families.

Being the Change within an Action-Centered Approach

It is unfortunate that Juliet was the only child who expressed an action-centered approach to spirituality because I wasn't able to compare her experiences to other children of the same style. What I was able to do, however, was examine what she believed to be important aspects of her spiritual life. While her opinions and values might have been slightly different than those of other action-centered children, I believe that key aspects of her spirituality can prove to be largely representative of children who share her spiritual style. Therefore, let's allow Juliet to en-lighten our views of an action-centered spirituality, especially as it affects the lives of children.

Juliet's spiritual life included a few characteristics that linked her to other spiritual styles. Like mystics, she valued an active prayer life through which she communicated with the transcendent God. What set her prayer life apart from children of other spiritual styles, however, was that her prayers were frequently responses to disaster and injustice. Instead of thanking God for her family, friends, church, and nature, she evoked the spirit of the Hebrew prophets and psalmists by crying out to God in lament over the injustices of the world and seeking guidance and assistance.

Juliet also exhibited a strong appreciation for worship expressed through music, like the children whose dominant spiritual style was marked by emotion. She said that singing in a Christmas pageant was a fond memory of her church experiences, and her mother told me that she loved to sing in the church's children's choir. During these times, Juliet was able to experience God in ways that left lasting impressions in her memory.

The third spiritual characteristic that Juliet held in common with children from another style was a focus on the Bible and learning about God, which revealed the speculative nature of her spiritual style. Even though she only took six out of a possible twenty-five photographs, two of them were pictures of her Bible. Clearly, she was determined to capture a clear image of her Bible. The importance she placed on learn-ing about God was further demonstrated by the fact that she thought a characteristic that made the building a church was that the congregation discussed and interpreted the Bible together. For her, the Bible was of vital importance as a basis and guide for her thoughtful and active faith.

These three characteristics—an active prayer life, a love of musical worship, and an emphasis on the Bible—likened Juliet's spirituality to those of other styles. Perhaps through these emphases and qualities, she was demonstrating a degree of balance between her dominant action-centered approach and other spiritual styles. Perhaps she connected these qualities to her desire for justice in the world. Whatever the reason, we must take such characteristics seriously and ensure these aspects are present in our ministries with children.

When it comes to the qualities of her spirituality that were critical and relatively unique to her spiritual style, three repeatedly surfaced during our conversations and exercises. First, Juliet expressed a deep appreciation for her church's intergenerational community, which her mother confirmed by disclosing how much she loved to worship and volunteer alongside diverse groups of Christians. Juliet was empowered when she was surrounded by many fellow Christ-followers who could encourage, inspire, and care for one another, as Christ first cared for them. In Juliet's own words, this community was important because there were "lots of people that take care of you if anything happens." She could enjoy time at her church because she had a sort of "extended family"[17] in her faith community that looked out for her. For those people who are determined to change the world, such a community can provide necessary and continual support.

While she appreciated knowing that she was cared for, Juliet's action-centered spiritual style was most vividly expressed and nurtured through the care she showed to others, especially through acts of social justice. Her favorite memory at her church was helping with a free meal for homeless people because this experience gave her satisfaction knowing that "I'm helping the homeless and it's really fun doing it at the same time." Through her involvement in Operation Christmas Child, she was able to feel close to God and encounter the God of justice in ways that left lasting impressions on her life.

Although filling a shoe box for a child in an impoverished country was great for the time being, it might have proven to be insufficient in the long run. Juliet had a strong desire to go to Africa on a mission trip and would have rather been out helping people across the ocean

17. Allen, "Nurturing Children's Spirituality in Intergenerational," 270.

than sitting in Sunday school or worship services. To quote her mother, "she's starting to realize that what she learns [at church] needs to have some sort of impact in what she does." Her faith was incomplete unless it was put into action in order to break down the social injustices that hold people in bondage and limit them from living fulfilling and dignified lives.

For Juliet, being in a local community and acting for the betterment of the global community were expressed and demonstrated through the practice of communion, a ritual that the children and adults at Lawrence Park celebrated together. She felt especially connected to God during communion. Even though she saw other people talking or moving about during this special time, Juliet made sure that she took time to pray "for what communion's about." For her, the sacrifice of Jesus wasn't to be taken lightly and it influenced the sacrifices that she made in order to help others.

I'm fascinated that Juliet was the only child with an action-centered approach to spirituality, and that she was the only child of color to be involved in the focus groups. Perhaps Juliet had experienced social injustices first-hand as a person with African roots and this motivated her to fight injustice. Maybe she was raised hearing the stories of her ancestors' trials and tribulations and she refused to allow other people to treat their fellow human beings with the cruelty with which her ancestors were treated. While I can't be certain that Juliet's African roots prompted her, whether consciously or unconsciously, to live out her spirituality through action, I would be shocked to discover that this did not affect her spiritual style.

The words and experiences of these thirteen young people clearly show that children experience God and encounter the holy in very different manners. All the children had personal signatures to their spirituality, unique ways in which they expressed this innate quality of their lives. But, as we have seen, four distinct ways of knowing God emerged within this diversity—words, emotion, symbols, and action.

In this chapter, we have traversed deeper into the realm of spiritual styles by exploring how these four ways of knowing God were etched onto the lives and experiences of these children. Through their willingness to share about their inner lives, we have been granted a peek at how spiritual styles affect how children encounter God, experience their congregations, and make sense of the world around them.

We've seen that the ministries and practices that nurture these children differ as we move from style to style, demonstrating the importance of moving beyond one-size-fits-all approaches to nurturing children's spirituality. Pastors, parents, and teachers can use ministry models, methods, and practices that engage children of each and every spiritual style in authentic, life-changing trans/formation. In the next few chapters we'll move from our discussion of what spiritual styles are and how they are manifested in children's lives to an exploration of how pastors, parents, and other adults can create environments that welcome, include, and nurture all children.

5

Welcome

A Strategy for Including All Children

CHRISTIAN EDUCATOR MICHAEL ANTHONY believes that human beings "come to experience God and learn about him in unique and personal ways."[1] While this may be the case, the different ways in which people experience God can be categorized into four groups or styles of spirituality: word, emotion, symbol, and action. By affirming and embracing all four spiritual styles, congregations, pastors, teachers, and parents can more effectively nurture the spirituality of the children in their care. This is done through the creation of environments that are harmoniously dissonant, that is, spaces that speak to children of every spiritual style so as to allow each and every young person to feel a sense of fit while challenging them to reach beyond their dominant style.

In an essay published a few years ago, Joyce Bellous makes an important statement: "Children cannot flourish unless they fit to a satisfying degree. . . . A feeling of fit is important for spiritual growth."[2] Therefore, it is vital for churches to intentionally work to create environments in which children of all spiritual styles are included and experience a sufficient degree of fit. Bellous continues, "Inclusive teachers [and churches] provide for the study of words, so that children become precise and make cognitive gains; offer opportunities to learn through feeling and open up occasions for telling personal stories and explaining what they mean, using the arts; allow time for silence, wonderment and imagination to set the agenda for interpreting experience; and bring children into set-

---

1. Anthony, "Putting Children's Spirituality," 33.
2. Bellous, "Five Classroom Activities," 100.

tings where they can take specific, focused action aimed at improving the world."[3]

Unfortunately, the testimonies of the thirteen children who spoke with me about their spiritual lives demonstrate that, although churches may attempt to create environments conducive to spiritual trans/formation and experiences, many miss the mark and fail to include all children. As a result, young disciples who do not feel as though they are welcomed and included are at risk of keeping their spiritual experiences private and of robbing others of the richness that comes through spiritual diversity.[4] Such young people might also believe that something is wrong with them, since everyone else may seem to belong and fit within the faith community. Making room for all children is vital for inviting every child to participate in the metaphorical dance of spiritual trans/ formation, even if the steps they know are different from one another.

Let me exemplify this using the children's ministries of Lawrence Park Presbyterian Church and Northview Community Church. Lawrence Park, with its artwork, rituals, and symbolism, its focus on biblical teaching through sermons, lessons, and children's messages, its emphasis on music and worship, and its opportunities to serve the community, seems to have created an environment that is inclusive of all four spiritual styles. As such, the children from this faith community expressed high degrees of love and appreciation for their congregation and spoke fondly of their experiences with God at this church. And while a diverse environment such as Lawrence Park includes all children, it also helps to ensure that the children don't move too far toward an extreme version of their dominant style. This is a harmoniously dissonant congregation, one that brings together different (and even opposing) ways of knowing God in a manner that nurtures and challenges each person toward growth. In a paradoxical way, dissonance allows harmony to be achieved.

Northview Community Church, on the other hand, primarily ministers to children who express their spiritual lives through emotion. While Abigail was reasonably content with her church experiences, Caleb expressed dissatisfaction toward the lack of mystery surrounding God in the church's teaching and Ben didn't seem to have his word-centered spirituality nurtured by Northview's ministries. The spiritual elements that mattered most to these boys were not included in their

3. Ibid., 102.
4. Ibid.

church's ministries. This left them to find alternative ways to know God and express their spiritual lives.

While both of these congregations certainly value their children, only one of them has created an environment that shows all children that they are valued by helping them to sense that they belong, fit, and are included. In order to effectively minister to the spiritual needs of all children—by both nurturing their dominant style and challenging it with diversity—it's important for congregations to develop spaces, programs, and leaders that include and nurture young people of all spiritual styles and provide all children with a sense of fit.

Creating genuinely inclusive environments can be difficult work. As with most challenging tasks, it is helpful to create both long-term objectives and short-term goals to bring about the desired results of an environment of inclusivity. In *Welcoming Children*, practical theologian Joyce Mercer discusses the importance of forming and utilizing both strategies and tactics in order to transform ministries from places of individualistic consumption to places of authentic spiritual trans/formation. In explaining her use of these two terms, she writes,

> strategies are longer-term plans, made by those who have the luxury of time for analysis and contemplation of the "big picture." Strategies are used by those who are relatively well-positioned in a conflict or struggle, who have the time to reflect and make the connections between the situation as it stands and the changes and outcomes desired. Tactics, on the other hand, are the activities of people from the underside of a struggle. They have neither the luxury of time nor perhaps the benefit of a thoroughgoing look at the situation as a whole.... Tactics are necessarily shorter-term actions, but they can have considerable impact.[5]

For churches to develop environments in which all children, regardless of their spiritual style, feel a sense of inclusivity and fit, tactics and strategies must both be intentionally employed.

In this chapter, as well as the next one, I speak as a person who has "the luxury of time for analysis and contemplation of the 'big picture.'"[6] In these two chapters, I offer overviews of what I believe to be two important, broad strategies for creating harmoniously dissonant spiritual environments in which all children can be welcomed, valued, and in-

5. Mercer, *Welcoming Children*, 196.

6. Ibid.

cluded, as well as appropriately challenged toward growth. In the present chapter, I focus on what it means to welcome children into the wider faith community and seek to include them in the life of the church. In the next chapter, I explore how story can serve as an overarching strategy for the spiritual trans/formation of all children, regardless of their dominant spiritual style.

In the seventh chapter, I transition from strategies to tactics, from the view of analysis and contemplation about what might work best to the view on the frontlines of children's ministry. The many tactics that I present can be effective for ministering to children of each specific spiritual style. While it's not likely that every tactic will nurture children of every style to the same degree, it is vital that readers remember that tactics geared toward children of different styles can constructively challenge them to keep a sense of balance in their spiritual lives as well as a respect for diversity.

Since tactics are often formed by those on the "underside" of a situation or struggle, chapter 7 relies heavily on the voices of my thirteen young friends. Their spiritual lives, as presented in chapters 3 and 4, form the basis for the ideas and resources that I offer. Yet I also draw from the work of those who have come before me: my colleagues in the world of children's ministry. In this way, I allow the voices of those on the frontlines—children and practitioners—to speak about how churches can meet the spiritual needs of children from each spiritual style. The ideas, concepts, and practices offered in these chapters are meant to serve as springboards for creating contextually-appropriate ministries with children. Let's begin by exploring the first strategy that can nurture the spirituality of all children regardless of their dominant style.

WELCOMING AND INCLUDING CHILDREN
IN THE COMMUNITY OF FAITH

The day that I am writing these words is the sixteenth day of the Hebrew month of Nisan. This means that today is the second day of Passover, the Jewish festival commemorating the Exodus from Egypt and God's liberation of the Israelites from slavery. As I think about the importance of Passover, which can pass by each year unnoticed by many Christian communities, I recall the important role that children play in the celebrations of this special eight-day festival.

On at least one evening during Passover week, Jews are to hold a Seder, a ritual feast that celebrates the freedom from slavery that God granted to the ancient Israelites. In this commemorative meal, children play a crucial role. Throughout the evening, the youngest child raises a series of questions that invite the host of the Seder to recount, with emotion and physical reenactment, the Exodus of the Hebrew people from Egyptian slavery. One important question is "Why is this night different from other nights?" Without the asking of these questions by the youngest child, this feast lacks the essential narrative that sets it apart from other days of the Jewish calendar. Children have a pivotal role in this festival and it's necessary for them to be a part of the community that celebrates their faith tradition.

We Christians have much to learn from our Jewish friends. Rather than seeing children as integral to the community of faith, we sometimes exclude them from the community's core and defining practices and break them up into segregated age groups. While many congregations have good intentions for these practices, like providing children with "age-appropriate" learning, they don't always consider the negative effects that age segregation can have not only on the children, but on the entire faith community.

In her posthumously published book, Letty Russell makes an important point about inclusion in the church: "Until all are included equally, the ecclesiastical body of Christianity remains broken."[7] Although she was speaking primarily about women, Russell reminds us that the church cannot be whole when anyone is excluded from its practices and from the wider faith community. Women, the elderly, immigrants, disabled persons, and children—all are called to be a part of the body of Christ. As the instructions for Jewish feast days contained in the Hebrew Bible remind us, God intends children to be an integral part of faith communities. Let's explore how churches can welcome and include children in their congregations and why such practices are so crucially important for the spiritual trans/formation of children of all spiritual styles.

7. Russell, *Just Hospitality*, 17.

THE IMPORTANCE OF INCLUDING CHILDREN
IN THE COMMUNITY OF FAITH

In *Offering the Gospel to Children*, Gretchen Wolff Pritchard prophetical-ly states, "Adults come to church on Sunday in order to worship; children come to Sunday school to acquire information."[8] A result of this Sunday segregation is an epidemic that has swept across western Christianity. Rather than being granted access to trans/formative experiences within the wider Christian community, children are escorted to the basement where they can be a part of a program that aims at instilling information in them. Consider Townsend Baptist Church, where children can get to the basement through a separate entrance to the building.

Models of children's ministry consisting solely of segregated, "age-appropriate" teaching are based on the production line and greenhouse paradigms, which were presented in chapter 1. What such models deem most important for children is the acquisition of specific data and infor-mation in environments that are intentionally set apart for their growth. Religious education is certainly important for children, but, as Pritchard states, it's "no substitute for real, living membership in the community of faith."[9] Although there are appropriate times and places for segregated, age-appropriate educational ministries, such programs often take prece-dence over the vital practices of the faith community that link us with the myriad of Christians throughout the world and throughout history. Failing to include children in the community of faith can have dramatic negative effects on both the children and the wider community.

Many scholars, practitioners, and parents agree that the spiritual life of children can be nurtured through close, personal relationships with caring adults. The research that I undertook confirms this. Some children, such as Caleb, Laurie, and Nicholas, were profoundly influ-enced and affected by the guidance of their parents and other family members. Others, such as Megan, Abigail, and Houston, received a great deal of spiritual nurture from particular non-parent adults within their congregations. Clearly, children can receive important spiritual guidance and direction from the adults in their lives who make an effort to get to know them and allow themselves to be known in return.

8. Pritchard, *Offering the Gospel*, 140–41.
9. Ibid., 141.

Unfortunately, George Barna has discovered that although individuals within the faith community can have a strong impact on children, they usually make up the third tier of influence in the life of the child. He holds that the strongest tiers of influence in a child's life are usually (1) the child's parents, which is a good thing, and (2) the media (movies, video games, the Internet, music, advertising) and peers.[10] The movies children watch, the music that pumps through their iPods, and the video games that they play have a greater influence on young people than their faith communities. Although it's possible for children to be significantly influenced by congregations, a strong influence from churches is relatively unusual. But this can change!

Rise Up, Hungarians, Your Country Calls[11]

Let me illustrate the trans/formative power of inclusion and welcome with a personal anecdote. When my sister, Ann, was in the fourth grade, she was part of a local Brownie chapter (the junior division of the Girl Guides). One of the assignments that her leader gave her was to research her ethnic heritage. She chose to research the Hungarian roots of our father. Thanks to this project, my family discovered the Sudbury Hungarian Society, a local Hungarian group focused on preserving our ethnic heritage by building relationships with one another, by engaging in practices within the Hungarian culture, and by learning about elements of the culture: dance, music, food, festivals, and language (did I mention the food?).

This community, in which I was heavily involved from the first grade through the end of high school, had an incredible trans/formative influence on the lives of my family members. Through our participation in this group, my sister and I became proud to call ourselves Hungarian and we readily invited our friends, regardless of their ethnicity and heritage, to learn about Hungarian folklore and participate in the community. We went from having Hungarian roots to *being* Hungarian. Even my French-Canadian mother proudly displays a plaque that attests to her involvement in the community as an "honorary Hungarian."

10. Barna, *Transforming Children*, 57–58.

11. This heading is taken from Petőfi Sándor's famous poem, "Nemzeti Dal," or "National Song." Petőfi, "National Song," 319. Thank you to Laszlo Peczeli for ensuring that the English translation of this poem that I learned as a child was indeed accurate.

Such identity formation didn't come about because as children my sister and I only met with other children in the Hungarian group and engaged in cognitive knowledge-acquisition about Hungarian culture and history. The reason that the influence of this community of practice was so powerful was because we were significant contributors to its life. We had conversations with people of all ages. We danced next to men and women thirty years older than us. We performed on our citeras (a Hungarian musical instrument) in front of the entire community. During special occasions, the whole group ate together, sharing stories and reminiscing about past trips and events. These practices allowed Ann and me (as well as our parents) to move from data acquisition to identity formation through genuine participation in the community. Not only did we learn *about* Hungarian culture, but we were socialized into the Hungarian way of life.

The aspect of the group that was most difficult to maintain was Hungarian language lessons, for this was the time focused on acquiring specific knowledge through classes rather than engaging in the defining practices of the group and the Hungarian people. It wasn't until we travelled to Hungary with the group and *experienced* the language that learning some Hungarian words began to matter.

Thanks to my family's involvement in this community, I'm proud to call myself Hungarian, and I expressed my gratitude for this community at my wedding. As I stood at the front of our church, waiting for the doors at the back to open and for my bride to walk down the aisle, I looked around at the sea of faces and saw many members of the Hungarian group who had made the six-hour trek from Sudbury to join me on this special day. And afterwards, we celebrated with traditional Hungarian food, music, and dancing at the local Hungarian hall!

This story of my family's involvement in the Sudbury Hungarian Society mirrors the power that faith communities can have in the lives of young disciples. Instead of relegating children to their own spaces apart from the wider faith community, congregations are called to welcome children into the core community, teach them what it means to be Christian, allow them to engage in defining practices, and help them to foster relationships with Christians of all ages. When these elements are present, the faith community can become a strong trans/formative influence in the lives of children and help to shape their identities as members of the church. While making gains in one's knowledge is certainly important, it alone cannot allow children to form identities as community members. Rather than allowing television and video games to be the secondary tier of influence in their children's lives (after their parents), faith communities that truly welcome and include children can become a powerful stimulus of trans/formation. They can help young people to commit themselves to God and one another and form identities as children of God and members of the body of Christ.

The Water That Divides Us (But Doesn't Need To)

At some point in this conversation about including children in the faith community, it seems necessary for me to address a topic that has, at times, been unpleasant and divisive among Christians of differing traditions: baptism. In particular, the issue is often defined as infant baptism versus believer's baptism.

It's not remotely possible for me (or any other lone individual) to bridge this divide, heal past wounds caused by it, and provide a definitive answer about the proper time of baptism. Yet I would like to address both forms of baptism and demonstrate how one's views of this rite of passage can encourage a community to include children in their defining practices.

In the recent edited volume, *Nurturing Children's Spirituality*, two scholars provide excellent theological views of childhood from their church traditions. Speaking from the Presbyterian position, Timothy Sisemore discusses the importance of infant baptism for Reformed communities. For people of this tradition, baptism acts as a sign that the child is a member of the covenant community and the church, and has received the forgiveness of sins.[12] In light of this, Sisemore argues that in communities in which infant baptism is practiced, including Lawrence Park Presbyterian Church, children are welcomed to participate in the worship of the congregation.[13] The sign of baptism means they are part of the community and must be treated as whole, active, and contributing members. Baptism is the means through which children are initially welcomed in the community.

Immediately after Sisemore's chapter, Holly Allen offers a discussion of theological perspectives of children from the view of communities that

---

12. Sisemore, "Reformed and Presbyterian," 103.
13. Ibid., 106.

practice adult or believer's baptism, like Townsend and Northview. The forerunners of some of these traditions were Anabaptists (literally "re-baptizers") who held that baptism should be reserved for those who can consciously believe, confess to be a member of the church, and submit themselves to the community's discipline and discipleship.[14] Therefore, rather than baptizing infants, many of the traditions that take their lead from Anabaptism—whether or not they're still part of the Anabaptist family—practice infant or child dedication, a celebration in which the parents and faith community dedicate their child to God and promise to do all they can to raise the child "in the training and instruction of the Lord" (Eph 6:4). This practice is reminiscent of Jesus' dedication at the temple in the second chapter of Luke's gospel.

Although these congregations don't welcome children into the community through infant baptism, Allen argues that children, by virtue of the radical grace of God, ought to be seen as important members of the faith community and should be intentionally welcomed and included. She writes, "Probably nothing will foster children's relationship with God more than their being among adults who hold them, lay hands on them, bless them, and pray for them and with them. Nurturing children of the church toward the time when they will commit their lives to Christ requires, more than anything else, a faith community where children and committed adult believers are regularly and intentionally *together*."[15]

Speaking from different views of the role of baptism, these two scholars agree that children ought to be seen as important members of the faith community and should be welcomed and cherished as such. Whatever Christian tradition we may follow, whether we practice infant or believer's baptism, the inclusion of children is more than appropriate—it is vital to their spiritual trans/formation. And it's crucial to the life of the whole community.

Children as Gifted Image-Bearers

Welcoming children in the wider faith community and including them in its life isn't only advantageous for young people. The larger body of believers can also reap the benefits of having children contribute to the life of the community. As active, spiritual, faith-filled makers of mean-

14. Allen, "Anabaptist/Believers Church," 113. Yoder, *Anabaptism*, 274.
15. Allen, "Anabaptist/Believers Church," 124.

ing, children are capable of genuinely contributing to the life of the congregation.

God gives children unique abilities and talents that can be overlooked and neglected by adults. By inviting young people into the wider faith community, adults find themselves in prime positions to witness the wonderful gifts that God has bestowed on even the youngest of those who are made in God's image. But if children are separated from the larger body of believers, churches can neglect the gifts and talents that God has given to be used to further God's kingdom. How can children's gifts be utilized when they are removed from the life of the faith community and taught that they must pass through a series of age-segregated classes in order be a true part of the church?

Furthermore, as whole human beings, children are made in God's image and reveal God's characteristics. Yes, they can be noisy, messy, candid (sometimes too candid for our liking), and inappropriate, at least according to cultural norms and standards of conduct. And sometimes their vulnerability might require more care than we're willing to offer. But isn't the God in whose image children are made also messy, noisy, candid, inappropriate (according to our standards), and even vulnerable? These attributes of children that we often like to ignore and suppress are actually gifts that young people offer to us and can help us to know God.

One church in the United States includes even young infants in the community and gives them a vital role. Whenever a baby cries, the church is reminded to pray for those children around the world who are in need yet whose cries go unheard. By excluding children from the faith community, congregations may limit the capacity of young people to reveal God's character, they can miss children's witness to the fullness of a species created in God's image, and they can rob children of roles that only they can play.

PRACTICES OF WELCOME AND INCLUSION

Now that we have seen the importance of including children in the life of the faith community, I can imagine (and hope) that some readers might wonder how they can begin to embrace children as part of their church's life through practices of welcome and inclusion. In the rest of this chapter, I examine three general approaches to ministry that can help congregations to welcome and include children in the wider faith community. While each approach possesses a degree of overlap with the others, I break them apart to make them easier to understand. In this way, I provide three conceptual blueprints for including children in the faith community.

From the Sidelines to Center Field

In order for members of a faith community to experience trans/formative growth, they must engage in practices that foster learning and help build identities as community members. But such learning isn't simply the acquisition of facts and data. It is so much more. It's a gradual process of socialization and identity formation characterized by the increasing ability to perform functions that allow a person to be a full and genuine participant in the community. But in order for such trans/formation to occur in the lives of community members, they must engage in practices of legitimate peripheral participation.[16]

This approach to learning, which can be vividly seen through the ministry of Jesus,[17] posits that people form their identities through participation in a community of practice. This means that congregations who wish to help children build identities as members of the Christian community should grant them access to the trans/formative and defining practices of the community, whether they be acts of service, Scripture reading, communion, musical corporate worship, or other rituals that make up the identity of the community. Such participation is dialectical (it goes back and forth): "participation in social communities shapes our experience, and it also shapes those communities; the transformative potential goes both ways."[18]

In welcoming children to participate in the life of the faith community, churches must be open to the changes and shifts that can occur by having children be a part of the wider congregation. Congregations are often tailored to the needs of adults, so it takes a lot of work to invite children to truly be a part of a faith community. It might forever change the shape and vision of a congregation. But these changes, while they

16. Legitimate peripheral participation is an approach to education and learning that was spearheaded by Jean Lave and Etienne Wenger. See Lave and Wenger, *Situated Learning*.

17. For an examination of how legitimate peripheral participation can be seen in the teaching and ministry of Jesus, see Csinos, "'Come, Follow Me.'"

18. Wenger, *Communities of Practice*, 56–57.

may be difficult at first, can make the church into a place in which God's radical hospitality is offered to all people.

In order for the participation of children to be trans/formative, it must be legitimate and, at first, peripheral. Legitimacy refers to the community's authentic sponsorship of the newcomers who, for our purposes, are children. Speaking of such sponsorship, Joyce Mercer writes that, "for children to gain an identity as members in the community of practice, they must have access not only to its edges but also to its core, in the form of access to its centrally defining practices."[19] This means that children, with their stumbling and inexperience, are community members and as such ought to be given legitimate access to participate in the community's core practices. In doing so, stumbling and mistakes are transformed from hindrances into opportunities for learning and growth.[20] And in the process, both the young child and the experienced church elder are welcomed as legitimate members of the congregation.

Furthermore, the children's participation must be peripheral and should gradually lead to full participation. Children and other newcomers shouldn't necessarily be seen as full participants, for they're still learning what it means to be a member of the community. Although such peripherality may be perceived as negative, this concept is actually positive because it allows learning and trans/formation to occur in ways that are appropriate to one's understanding and experience. As a person's experience and knowledge increases, so does his or her access to core practices. Children can begin on the sidelines, as participant-observers who watch what it means to be members of the community. Gradually, they can engage in simple and then more complex tasks. Finally, when ready, they can become full members who help shape the community at its very core. And throughout this entire process, they are valued as legitimate community members.

Let me illustrate this concept by discussing how it can be used during communion. While it may be inappropriate for very young children to partake of the elements of communion, it's beneficial for them to be present for this ritual. As they grow and continue to learn, there will come a time when it is quite appropriate for them to join the congregation in eating bread and drinking wine or juice. Over time, their learning and trans/formation continues as their level of participation increases.

19. Mercer, *Welcoming Children*, 201.
20. Wenger, *Communities of Practice*, 101.

Perhaps these people, who are no longer seen as newcomers, can one day help to lead the congregation in the practice of communion by distributing the elements. As their experience and knowledge grow, so does their participation in the community's rituals and practices, which in turn increases their experience and knowledge. And the results of such legitimate peripheral participation can be trans/formative for the entire community.

Enabling children to be legitimate participants in congregations allows them to witness and experience the myriad of practices that define faith communities. They can observe how others engage in the core rituals and defining practices like communion until one day they too can eat and drink the elements and even serve communion to their fellow congregants. In this way, children become apprentices of the faith community and learn to form identities as community members. But in order for such trans/formation to occur, it's important for children to be welcomed and included in the life of the faith community as legitimate peripheral participants.

Doing Life Together

As I mentioned earlier in this chapter, Lawrence Park Presbyterian Church stood out from Northview and Townsend by welcoming and including children from all four spiritual styles. This led the five children from this church to express a relatively high degree of appreciation for how the community of faith nurtures their spiritual lives. Because of this, Lawrence Park became an environment that was conducive to having spiritual encounters with God.

While some children from Northview and Townsend seemed to enjoy their children's programs, they didn't show the love and appreciation for their congregations that was evident in the young people from Lawrence Park. What was Lawrence Park doing that allowed Houston, Gordon, Juliet, Ian, and Freddy to express a love and appreciation for their faith community and to have important spiritual experiences within this congregation? I believe that one answer to this question lies in the practices that the entire faith community, including children, do together.

All faith communities have key practices that define who they are. When my wife and I lived in Richmond, Virginia, we attended a small congregation that had a number of more typical defining practices—

musical worship, communion, and preaching—as well as several other unique ones—sharing our joys and concerns, responding to sermons through questions and thoughts, lighting candles to represent our prayers, and sharing good food at potlucks.

One of the reasons I loved this community was because the children in the congregation were invited and encouraged to engage in these defining practices with the rest of the community. They led hymns on the piano and violin, shared about the struggles in their lives, and lit candles for their loved ones. And when we shared a meal, there was no "kids' table." Everyone who was present—whether three years old or seventy years old, pastor or newcomer—was invited to contribute to the life of the community.

A particular practice that has become meaningful to this congregation occurs every year near All Saints' Day. On the Sunday nearest to this day, everyone in the church is invited to bring in and share something that reminds them of the saints—living or dead—in their lives. From the young child who briefly showed a photo of her grandparents to the middle-aged man who brought a letter from a dear friend, people of all ages celebrate together the individuals who have made a difference in their lives.

On a particular Sunday, one young girl went to the top floor of the old house-turned-Civil-War-hospital-turned-church in which we met, grabbed a beanbag chair, and dragged it downstairs during the middle of the sermon. She dropped it in the aisle, plopped down in it, and joined us in taking in our pastor's preaching. I even recently heard that the congregation adopted a new intergenerational practice: watching episodes of a popular TV series and theologically reflecting on the show through group discussion. Through these many practices and an appreciation for the gifts that people of all ages brought to them, all members of this church were able to do life together, to join one another on the spiritual journey.

While it may have some practices that are more unusual than other congregations, our church in Richmond is not distinctive in the fact that it has practices that are central to its life. For many faith communities, including the three involved in this study, baptism, communion, preaching, and corporate worship are four defining practices. As a downtown parish, Lawrence Park also finds its congregational identity through its ministry and service to the poor of the neighborhood. Such defining practices shouldn't be taken lightly, for they form the very core of what it means to be a member of the faith community.

At Lawrence Park, children are openly and enthusiastically invited into the community's defining practices. They celebrate communion with the entire congregation. They serve their neighborhood alongside a diverse group of people. They are present for various special events. They participate in aspects of corporate worship, sometimes even providing leadership. They join the congregation in welcoming children into the covenant community through the rite of baptism. As the children and adults of Lawrence Park share these practices with one another, both the identity of the community and the identities of individual members are trans/formed. By engaging in such practices within the wider faith community, the five children from Lawrence Park have come to know that they are valued members of their congregation. Whether they realize it or not, these children are legitimate peripheral participants.

Churches that treat children according to the third concept I presented in chapter 1—as fellow spiritual pilgrims—can't fully embrace this paradigm while excluding their youngest congregants from the community's core practices. Central to this paradigm is the assertion that ministry is not *to* or *for* children. Ministry happens *with* children. It counters banking concepts of education and, like the Sudbury Hungarian Society and our congregation in Richmond, it values the importance of having children engage in the whole of the community. It affirms that "Christian knowing arises from reflection on one's own experience in relationship with the Christian community experience."[21] How can ministry *with* children that brings about such knowing occur when children aren't present to engage in congregational practices with the rest of the faith community? In short, it can't happen.

Of the four spiritual styles, none is more important or better suited to Christian living and trans/formation than any of the others. Each one provides a different, legitimate avenue through which individuals and communities can experience God in personal and corporate ways. As I have noted, however, a healthy balance between the four styles must be present, or congregations and individual members risk falling into one of the dangerous aberrations that come with a strong dominance of one style over the others. One way that children can develop such a balance, while receiving affirmation for their dominant spiritual style, is by being

21. Groome, *Christian Religious Education*, 147.

involved in a community that exists within a harmoniously dissonant balance or tension.

Christian educators can attest to the fact that children "imitate the actions of those around them."[22] If children are separated from the wider faith community and only engage with one or two adults, they most likely will begin to imitate the dominant spiritual styles of those few people. This seemed to be true in the case of Nicholas, whose mother and father both appeared to have a word-centered approach to spirituality. Because they homeschooled him using a faith-based curriculum, much of his spiritual life was dominated by word-centered tasks and goals. It was not surprising, then, that his spiritual style was dominated by words.

Situations such as this can have negative effects. First, children who possess the same style as the few adults in their lives—whether parents or pastors—can begin to see their style as the correct way of knowing God, and they can slip into the extreme form of that spiritual style. After all, they have no (or at least few) close adults modeling alternative ways to know God.

Conversely, children who possess a dominant style that differs from their leaders and parents may come to see their primary way of experiencing God as wrong or incomplete. Without close adults to demonstrate that the style they share is a legitimate way of encountering God, children may inappropriately and uncritically imitate the adults in their lives who possess different styles than they do. This can rob children of the joy that comes from having authentic experiences with God according to their own styles. Caleb may have been exceptional in that he understood that the problem was not him but the single-style approach of his faith community. Many other children in similar situations may believe that they are the problem.

Both of these possible situations—when children are surrounded by people of the same or those of different spiritual styles—can stifle a healthy spirituality and cause children to feel as though they don't fit within their congregation. They can feel excluded and they might even be led to believe that their experiences and relationships with God are problematic.

By engaging in the core practices of the wider faith community, children can be surrounded by adults who express all four spiritual styles. They can interact with people who value reading and interpreting

22. Yust, *Real Kids*, 149.

scriptural texts, as well as those who place importance on stamping out injustice. They can learn from people who use emotion to connect with God and those who sit in quiet contemplation, waiting to hear God's voice. An atmosphere of balance and diversity, of harmonious dissonance, allows children to experience all four ways of connecting with God and helps them to develop a healthy, balanced tension between all styles. But a harmoniously dissonant environment can't help children if they are excluded from the core practices of the faith community.

Action-Reflection

It has been thirty years since Thomas Groome published his groundbreaking book, *Christian Religious Education*, which James Fowler said was "Likely to be the most significant single book in the field of Christian education for the next twenty years."[23] Fowler's prediction was accurate. Groome's book is still of great significance for those interested in the spiritual trans/formation and education of followers of Jesus.

Central to Groome's work is the approach to Christian religious education that he refers to as *shared praxis*. Shared praxis requires educators and pastors to "see ourselves as brother or sister pilgrims in time *with* our students [and congregants]."[24] It is, therefore, quite appropriate to make use of such an approach within the paradigm of children as fellow spiritual pilgrims—active agents who encounter God and make meaning of their experiences amidst the world around them. Since the concept of shared praxis is developed by Groome throughout his nearly 300-page book, it's impossible for me to explain it in a few pages with all the depth and breadth that it deserves. I will, however, present a basic introduction to shared praxis because I believe it is as important for spiritual trans/formation today as it was when his book was first published in 1980. This overview is only meant to kindle your interest; I recommend a thorough study of Groome's work.

According to Groome, praxis is more than just practice, the opposite of theory. Praxis involves both practice *and* theory; they are two sides of the coin of praxis. It is the intentional and purposeful *reflection on one's reflection and action*. And the creative result of this reflection

23. Groome, *Christian Religious Education*, 1st ed., front cover.

24. Ibid., 137.

should lead to further action, reflection, and creation.[25] Shared praxis is an approach to spiritual trans/formation that oscillates between action and reflection. In Christian religious education, it's both a means and an end. We employ the active, reflective, and creative dimensions of praxis in order to engage in more active, reflective, and creative praxis.

So, what is *shared* praxis and what does this approach look like in a faith community? Groome describes it as "*a group of Christians sharing in dialogue their critical reflection on present action in light of the Christian Story and its Vision toward the end of lived Christian faith.*"[26] This approach to Christian religious education can be utilized with Christians of all ages (although it surely needs to be modified to the abilities of those who are engaging in it) to develop their identity through individual and communal reflection on God's ongoing story and the kingdom, or vision, of God. Done properly, this approach involves five key components:

- **Present Action**. This refers to more than one's thoughts and actions at the present moment. It's "whatever way we give expression to ourselves."[27] Our present action encompasses the entirety of our engagement with the world around us.

- **Critical Reflection**. This, the second component, can be summarized as "an activity in which one calls upon (1) critical reason to evaluate the present, (2) critical memory to uncover the past in the present, and (3) creative imagination to envision the future in the present."[28] Such reflection takes into account ways in which one has been shaped and how one makes meaning (reflecting on one's reflection) and involves remembering the past and imagining the future.

- **Dialogue**. The third component of shared praxis is an inter-subjective encounter between two or more people who speak and share the stories and visions upon which they have reflected. It involves the humility, vulnerability, and love that is reflected in subject-to-subject relationships of mutual care and respect. To

---

25. Groome, *Sharing Faith*, 136.

26. Groome, *Christian Religious Education*, 184.

27. Ibid.

28. Ibid., 185.

engage in genuine dialogue, all those present must love themselves, their fellow human beings, and the world around them.[29]

- **The Story**. Story, as it is used in shared praxis, is much more
  than a narrative or even our narratives. It is *"the whole faith tradition of our people however that is expressed or embodied."*[30] It is
  the great overarching story of God's interactions with the world
  and with humanity. It is the story that involves and envelops all
  members of the Christian community.

- **The Vision**. The vision to which Groome refers is the kingdom
  of God, which is God's good vision for the world. It is our lived
  "response to and God's promise in the Story, and the Story is the
  unfolding of the Vision."[31] This is the ultimate goal of shared
  praxis, and that of the entire Christian faith: that the kingdom of
  God becomes a fully-manifested living reality within the church
  and the world.

Take a breath. I know that all of this may seem convoluted; indeed,
it can be complicated. Let me pare away these components and offer a
minimalistic explanation of the five movements of shared praxis. Shared
praxis requires that we (1) name our present action, (2) tell, hear, and reflect on one another's stories, (3) dialogue with others about our stories,
(4) immerse ourselves in God's story, and (5) live out that story through
the vision of the kingdom of God.

Through this five-fold approach, all people, regardless of age and
spiritual style, are invited to reflect on their stories and experiences with
God and genuinely interact with those of others. It opens the door for
individuals to rub shoulders and make meaning with people of different
styles through honesty, vulnerability, and love. Shared praxis flattens the
spiritual terrain so that all those present, whether young or old, male
or female, word-centered or symbol-centered, stand on level ground. In
shared praxis, "There is neither Jew nor Greek, slave nor free, male nor
female, [old nor young], for you are all one in Christ Jesus" (Gal 3:28). It
invites people from all walks of life and who express all spiritual styles
to join together in action-reflection. It's no wonder that shared praxis

29. Groome, *Christian Religious Education*, 190.

30. Ibid., 192. For more about this story, see the section "The Story We Find Ourselves
In" in chapter 6.

31. Groome, *Christian Religious Education*, 193.

continues to be a respected approach to engaging people in spiritual trans/formation. Through it, people of all ages become active, present, and contributing members.

Welcoming children and making a place for them within the wider life of the faith community is an essential strategy for providing an environment that nurtures the spirituality of all children. It not only testifies to our love of young people, but also our love of Christ. It's so vital that David Jensen states, "if we do not welcome children, we cannot claim that we are following the Risen Lord."[32] To welcome children and include them in the life of the faith community is to welcome Christ and make room for him in congregational life. Indeed, in including children in our communities of practice, we include the risen Lord. Jesus said, "Whoever welcomes a little child like this in my name welcomes me" (Matt 18:5). Let us always have a place at the table for children.

32. Jensen, *Graced Vulnerability*, 130.

✿ 6

Story-Telling, Story-Hearing, Story-Living

A Strategy for Including All Children

SOME OF THE MOST cherished memories I have of my childhood involve my mom and dad putting me to bed at night. Often, as they were closing the drapes and tucking me in, I would ask them to tell me a story about their childhoods in rural southern Ontario. My father would recount tales of growing up on his family's tobacco farm—playing in the barn, helping to drive the tractors, and hiding in the back of the car while his older brother went to pick up a date. My mother used to tell me stories about walking along the train tracks with a toboggan as she and her friends made their way to a nearby hill for some mid-winter sledding.

One of my favorite bedtime stories was the story of the ceiling stars. When my mother was a girl, the ceiling of her bedroom was painted blue and covered with little gold stars—the kind we used to get in kindergarten for answering questions correctly or picking up after ourselves. Sometimes, when she awoke throughout the evening, my mother would look down at her bed and find it blanketed with fallen stars. She would call for my grandmother, who quietly came into her room with a stepladder, placed it near the edge of my mother's bed, climbed to the top step, and glued the fallen stars back onto the ceiling one by one.

These cherished tales of tobacco fields and ceiling stars aren't just stories about my parents, grandparents, aunts, and uncles. They are stories about me. They chronicle the people and places that had a hand in shaping who I am and who I am to become. These stories captured a piece of my innermost being and formed the core of my identity. And since I have lived in the house that my mother grew up in and I continue to visit it regularly, I'm continually reminded of these defining stories. If I look very closely, I can still see one small star caked under the white paint on the ceiling of the spare bedroom. I discovered this star when my wife and I were painting the walls of the room. It immediately transported me to a different time and the story became even more real than it had already been. This star is a reminder of where I have come from.

THE POWER OF STORY

Stories have a trans/formative power for people of all ages and spiritual styles. We are a storied people and good stories draw us into the narrative, tap into our deepest human needs—for love, affection, belonging, acceptance—and shape the core of who we are.

The contours of our identities are formed, for good or ill, through the rich narratives that we tell ourselves about our lives—about who we are, where we've come from, and how we find our places within the world. This is a central tenet of the field of narrative therapy, the founder of which wrote: "In striving to make sense of life, persons face the task of arranging their experiences of events in sequences across time in such a way as to arrive at a coherent account of themselves and the world around them. Specific experiences of events of the past and present, and those that are predicted to occur in the future, must be connected in a lineal sequence to develop this account. This account can be referred to as a story or self-narrative."[1]

Stories have the power to trans/form who we are. It makes sense, then, that faith communities make use of good stories of the faith tradition in order for children to hear about and identify with their spiritual ancestors and form identities as members of the community and tradition. Recognizing the trans/formative power of stories, Jack Seymour writes, "As stories are told, sacred traditions and meanings are being passed on to the next generation—stories of faiths, of families, of cultures, and of expectations for how the future is to be shaped so that all may live and flourish."[2]

Stories can be a wonderful way of tapping into children's inherent spirituality and helping them to have profound, creative, and unique experiences with God. This is true for children with a spirituality dominat-

1. White and Epston, *Narrative Means*, 10.
2. Seymour, "Tell Me a Story," 237.

ed by words or feelings as much as it is for those who are action-centered or symbol-centered. The power of stories transcends the boundaries of spiritual styles and touches the lives of all children. Indeed, narrative therapy holds that narrative strikes at the core of a person's self and can be a profound means of trans/formation. As Victoria Ford and Esther Wong note, "A story can be a powerful educational tool for both change and growth."[3] It is for this reason that the story strategy can be a powerful means for nurturing the spiritual lives of all children.

Regardless of one's dominant spiritual style, all children (and all people) can be trans/formed by the unique power of story. The stories that churches tell can shape and reshape the lives of their congregants. In this chapter, I speak of the story strategy, a way of connecting our stories with God's story in order to shape our lived experiences. But before turning our attention to just how this strategy can be used to nurture the spiritual lives of all children, we must first become informed about God's story.

THE STORY WE FIND OURSELVES IN[4]

Hebrew Bible scholar Walter Brueggemann believes that story "is our primal and most characteristic mode of knowledge. It is the foundation from which come all other knowledge claims we have."[5] When it comes to including children and helping them to be spiritually trans/formed, the power of story is without parallel.

Human beings shape and live their lives based on trans/formative narratives they believe to be true and through which meaning is made of their personal stories. As Craig Bartholomew and Michael Goheen write, "In order to understand our world, to make sense of our lives, and to make our most important decisions about how we ought to be living, we depend upon some story. . . . Individual experiences make sense and acquire meaning only when seen within the context or frame of some story we believe to be the true story of the world: each episode of our life stories finds its place there."[6]

---

3. Ford and Wong, *Narrative*, 311.
4. This heading is taken from McLaren, *Story*.
5. Brueggemann, *Creative Word*, 23.
6. Bartholomew and Goheen, *Drama of Scripture*, 18.

These trans/formative stories act as frames in which the pieces of our lives fit together; they are the lenses through which we see ourselves, others, and the wider world. And all of us hold to a dominant story through which we form our lives and find meaning in the world. Those looking to make a large profit in the business world may allow their lives to be shaped by the story of capitalism. Others, who seek the "American dream" to own a large, well-furnished house with granite countertops and marble floors, multiple luxury vehicles, and maybe even a white picket fence, might form their lives around stories of consumerism and materialism.

Christians, however, are called to be shaped by a particular story—the story of God's interactions with humanity. Although contained within the Christians Scriptures, this story began before humanity and continues today. It is, as Brian McLaren has called it, "the story we find ourselves in."[7] It is the living, ongoing tale of God's relationship with the world and with humanity. We who live and breathe on earth today are part of this story and continue to have a hand in shaping the chapters that have yet to be written. This story has the supernatural and transcendental power to shape and form human lives like no other narrative. In McLaren's words, it's "a beautiful, powerful, gritty story that resonates with, gives meaning to, and continues to unfold in the life and teaching of Jesus. And this story invites our participation as well, not as pawns on the squares of a cosmic chessboard, but as creative protagonists and junior partners with God in the story of creation."[8] It is this narrative in which we must immerse our children if we wish for them to be trans/formed by it as well.

A few years ago, a friend of mine began leading his church's senior high Sunday school. Upon first meeting the teens in his class, he took some time to get to know them and understand their present way of thinking about God and the Bible. He soon discovered that although these young people knew many of the individual stories in the Bible, they didn't comprehend how the stories fit together—or even that they were supposed to fit together—as part of God's story.

These young people are not unusual; I've witnessed time and time again how God's overarching story is dissected into small, stand-alone narratives in an attempt to teach them to children. Just as adults cut

7. McLaren, *Story.*
8. McLaren, *New Kind,* 47.

children's meat into small, easy-to-digest morsels, many tend to serve God's story in a similar fashion. VeggieTales videos are a prime example of this practice. Movies are available that loosely tell the tales of Queen Esther, David and Goliath, the Good Samaritan, and even Jesus' death and resurrection, with no attempt at linking these smaller, sub-stories to one another as part of the story of God.

This practice of chopping God's narrative into pieces robs the wider story of its profound trans/formative influence. Churches seeking to help children find their identities within their faith communities and traditions can begin to put God's story back together, explaining how God was at work from creation to the covenant, from the cross to consummation. Furthermore, children can begin to understand that this isn't just a story about other people. It's their story and they can have a hand in shaping how it continues to unfold. Churches can present the story in ways that encourage children to adopt it as their own and affirm with Brueggemann that "this is *my* story about *me*, and it is *our* story about *us.*"[9] Offering God's story to children starts them down a good and fruitful path.

After becoming unsettled with the story that he'd been taught for most of his life, Brian McLaren spent years trying to gain a sense of God's story as a wider, overarching, and ongoing narrative of God's interactions with humanity. He recounts: "it's not easy undoing many years of training in order to see the Bible with fresh eyes; the process took several years— and is still going on, actually."[10] It is important that churches present God's story to children so that, when they grow older, even though they might question and reexamine it, they need not go through the painstaking and unnerving process of unlearning and relearning.

STORY-TELLING, STORY-HEARING, STORY-LIVING

At this point, I anticipate that some readers may wonder what all of this means about ministry with children? How are we supposed to help children know God's story and make it their own story? What do we do to help children understand that they are part of God's story? What does the story strategy look like? I propose that this strategy has three key elements: story-telling, story-hearing, and story-living.

9. Brueggemann, *Belonging and Growing,* 31.
10. McLaren, *New Kind,* 46.

Story-Telling

When I was an undergraduate student, my wife (who was then my girl-friend) and I began an evening children's ministry program at our local congregation. Although this program ran simultaneously to a Sunday evening outreach service, a large proportion of children who attended belonged to church families. Most of the people who brought their children to these services were volunteers from our congregation rather than visitors. Upon realizing this, Jenny and I wanted to use this ministry to provide children with a space in which they could experience different ways of worshipping God.

Drawing from the ideas of Kathleen Chapman, we included a "worship moment" each week, during which time the children had an opportunity to focus their attention on God through a particular activity.[11] Sometimes we went on nature walks and conversed about the beauty of God's creation. At other times we wrote love letters to God expressing our thanks for all that God has done for us. But the most powerful worship moments were those in which we provided a time and place for children to tell their stories, to share with one another about what God has done and is doing in their lives.

The practice of allowing people to share their stories of God's involvement in their lives has been sustained in the church for thousands of years, from Miriam's song after crossing the Red Sea to African American spirituals. Also known as giving testimony, voicing personal stories about the work of God is a rich and trans/formative practice for adults and children alike. It offers freedom to the oppressed and sight to the blind.[12]

FREEDOM TO THE OPPRESSED

Let me begin by discussing the liberating power of stories, how they give freedom to the oppressed. In *Practicing Our Faith*, William Hoyt Jr. addresses the practice of testimony from the marginal experiences of African Americans. As a disadvantaged and oppressed people, African Americans make use of testimony—the telling of their stories—as a way of embodying their deepest emotions and needs.[13] Similarly, allowing children to speak the truth about their personal experiences of God

11. Chapman, *Teaching Kids*.
12. Jesus announced that his mission was to do likewise. See Luke 4:18.
13. Hoyt, "Testimony," 94–95.

provides them with a means through which they can receive affirmation and encouragement and work to become full members of the community of faith.[14] Fernando Cascante-Gómez, a Latin American Christian educator, promotes telling personal stories "form the underside" through countercultural autobiography, a practice that allows those who don't normally hold positions of power and status to offer "*an interpretive reading of the self during or after particular moments in life.*"[15] Indeed, stories offer freedom to the oppressed.

Our present North American culture, including many of today's churches, is ambivalent in its general view of childhood and this ambivalence negatively affects children.[16] Although people work to provide young people with the best health care, education, entertainment, and child care, the voices of many children continue to be drowned out by the more powerful voices of individualism, narcissism, materialism, and consumerism.

I recently observed such attitudes in a television commercial for personal video recording. As a father sits on his couch watching a hockey game late into the evening, his son pokes his head in from around the corner and says that he's having trouble sleeping. Looking somewhat annoyed at first, the father realizes that, through the miracle of personal video recording, he can pause the hockey game and take care of his son. He then rewinds the game and asks his son if he'd like to watch the last ten minutes with him. As they curl up on the couch together, the following words appear: "Pause TV. Not Life." It is as if the father wouldn't have been willing to care for his son if he hadn't been able to pause the hockey game. Although he's meant to come across as a loving father who creates a special moment to bond with his child, I wonder what would have happened if he hadn't been able to pause and rewind the game.

14. Hoyt, "Testimony," 94.

15. Cascante-Gómez, "Countercultural Autobiography," 282. The full definition of this practice is "the *interpretive reading of particular moments in the social life of a person who identifies himself or herself with a particular discriminated and/or dominated group in any given society. It is used as a way to voice unjust and oppressive realities suffered within institutional and societal contexts with the ultimate goal of promoting full social inclusion and social justice within and among co-existing diverse human communities.* More simply, countercultural autobiographies are stories from the underside of society meant as tools for education for justice and as invitations for transformative dialogue in institutional and societal settings" (286).

16. For an excellent exploration of ambivalence about children, see Mercer, *Welcoming Children.*

This television commercial is just one of many examples of how society speaks of the importance of children, while placing narcissistic and self-ish personal interests ahead of their needs.

Such an ambivalent view of childhood permeates North American culture. Yet more and more, Christians are realizing that the message of Jesus was (and continues to be) radically subversive and countercultural. It is meant to subvert the selfish, oppressive, and violent characteristics of society, including ambivalence toward children.[17] And this is still the mandate of the church. Providing children with a safe space, an open atmosphere, and a listening ear has become a countercultural activity, one that takes vulnerability on the part of the story-tellers and those who are part of the audience. It is an activity that provides freedom to the oppressed and a voice to the voiceless. It replaces a dangerous yet all-too-common ambivalence for children with a view that truly respects and values their stories and lives.

Sight to the Blind

Story-telling not only gives freedom to the oppressed, it also offers sight to the blind. In telling stories, people offer windows into their lives to those who are listening. People who listen to children's stories can learn about their inner lives, what they find meaningful and how they experience God and God's church.

Margaret Ann Crain understands the vital importance of hearing stories in order to understand others. "It reveals much of my identity, the 'who am I?' story . . . These stories carry my identity."[18] By allowing children to tell their stories, hearers receive a gift from children and give them a gift in return. "Telling their story provides [young people] with an opportunity to give something to others, an act, which in itself, acknowledges their value, significance and uniqueness."[19] The stories are gifts to the hearers and the immense pleasure, satisfaction, and value that come with story-telling are gifts to the story-teller. In this way, story-telling offers sight (and insight) to the teller and the hearer.

The first step for churches wishing to create spiritual environments in which every child fits is to provide them with forums in which they

---

17. For a discussion of the countercultural aspects of Jesus' encounters with children, see Csinos, "Biblical Theme."

18. Crain, "Reconsidering," 242.

19. Erickson, "Spirituality," 294.

can tell their stories and be heard by supportive members of the faith community—including other children. By making use of this important practice, congregations help children of all spiritual styles to know that no member of the congregation is voiceless, for all have infinite value and worth and are capable of shaping the community, whether they experience God through action, symbols, emotion, or words.

Through story-telling, mystics like Caleb can voice their concerns regarding the absence of mystery in Northview's teaching of God; action-centered children like Juliet can speak out for those in need of social justice; Megan and other young people of who focus on words can teach others about their views of God and the Bible; and children such as Houston, who express their spirituality through feelings, can testify (in song perhaps) about their emotional experiences of God. Through story-telling, all children, regardless of their dominant spiritual style, are given a legitimate voice and a harmonious dissonance between all styles can be maintained. They who have stories to tell, let them tell. They who have ears to hear, let them hear (Mark 4:9).

Story-Hearing

A second element of the story strategy involves hearing God's story. For pastors, parents, and ministry leaders, this means presenting children with the ongoing story of God's interactions with humanity. And although there are countless ways in which this story can be told, it's important to choose those that draw children into the story and let them walk around in it. After all, one of the goals of having children hear God's narrative is that they will eventually come to make it a story that is theirs, a story that is about them.

In order to have children "walk around" in God's story, some faith communities, including Lawrence Park Presbyterian Church, have transformed parts of their buildings into sets depicting places in the Bible. Lawrence Park used carpet tubes, gold paint, and curtains to turn an auditorium in their basement into Solomon's temple. They designed another room to transport children back to first-century Palestine. This space has murals depicting the land on which Jesus walked, complete with the Sea of Galilee painted on a wall. Other congregations in which I have been involved have created temporary sets that help children walk around in God's story. Using a painted canvas, ladders, tarps, and lighting, we transformed our church's youth room into caves, huts, and markets for special events and ministries with children.

At this point, readers might imagine that it would be difficult to find time in their overcrowded schedules and funds in their depleting budgets to design and create these structures for children. When I was on staff at congregations, I had the same thoughts! But through regional children's ministry networks, many churches pooled their resources and divided up work to bring these stories to life. These congregations staggered the schedules of their summer programs so that each one could have a week or two with the shared materials. By working together, several congregations enabled thousands of children to enter God's story through dramatic interpretations in make-shift biblical lands.

While building sets is certainly an exciting way to help children walk around in God's story, there are several other effective ways of helping children hear God's story, and many of the most effective ones are quite simple. One approach was so simple that my wife and I were not sure if it would capture the attention and interest of children at the Christian camp where we were working.

We'd been commissioned with the task of leading the children's program at a three-day camp on Labor Day weekend. Having grown up attending and volunteering at programs at this campground, my wife knew that these children were used to being entertained with mystifying illusions, energetic skits, and MTV-like music videos. Leaders at past programs had been full-time child evangelists, ministers, and program directors who traveled from camp to camp, bringing with them truckloads of professional equipment and assistants to help set up. We were two young students with a small budget and few resources at our disposal. There was no way that we could bring these children the glitter and glam that others had used before us. (And even if we could have, we probably wouldn't have.)

We decided to give the children something different from their other camp experiences. We chose to tell God's story through Jerome Berryman's imaginative approach to story-telling known as Godly Play.[20] Godly Play draws children into stories using simple props (such as wooden figures and pieces of fabric) in a calm, contemplative manner. At first, we were concerned about whether or not these energetic children would be drawn into these stories. But we thought we'd give it

20. Berryman, *Godly Play*.

a shot anyway. To our surprise, all the children present kept their eyes on the figures for the entirety of every story. Those who showed up late seemed to be angry with themselves for taking an extra lap around the campground on their bicycles and missing the beginning of the story.

We thought that Godly Play might provide balance to other programs at the camp by bringing symbolic and mystical elements to an environment filled with words and emotion. But to our surprise, this approach tapped into the spiritual lives of all the children who joined us in the children's pavilion. Through Godly Play, children of all spiritual styles were offered God's story in a way that opened their hearts and minds to wondering what this story means for their lives.

The ways that you might choose to help the children and families in your congregations to hear God's story will vary from context to context. What's important is to know God's story for yourself and offer it as a gift to the children in your midst. Only by hearing God's story can people make it their own.

Story-Living

Once children have told their stories and heard God's story, the final step of the story strategy is for them to make God's narrative their own, to *live into God's story*. This involves helping children to see that the stories they told one another and the story of God that they heard are connected in deep and intimate ways. It's about helping them see that God's narrative isn't just part of their stories, but that it is *their* story. It is a story about them. This is a goal of shared praxis, which we briefly explored in chapter 5. Groome's idea of the vision in shared praxis involves making God's story into our story so that we can faithfully shape how it unfolds in the world around us.[21] One way of helping children engage in story-living is through what Anne Streaty Wimberly calls "story-linking."[22]

In her book about African American religious education, Wimberly presents the concept of "story-linking." In her words, "Linking with our forebears' story helps to inspire us and to foster our commitment to continue on the Christian faith walk. . . . The task is to engage African Americans in story-linking in ways that help us reflect critically on our particular life stories in light of the Christian faith

21. Groome, *Christian Religious Education*, 193.
22. Wimberly, *Soul Stories*.

story."[23] Looking at children's spiritual trans/formation, religious educators such as Karen-Marie Yust have recognized the value of Wimberly's ideas for ministry with children. Indeed, story-linking can lead to story-living. It can help people see how their stories intersect with and are shaped by God's story.

But what exactly is story-linking? Wimberly offers a fine definition of this approach to religious education: "story-linking is a process whereby we connect parts of our everyday stories with the Christian faith story in the Bible."[24] In this way, the faith story acts as a mirror through which we see our own actions in the world.[25] Through linking the stories of everyday life with the story of the living God, we make meaning of our narratives in new ways. But this is easier said than done. It involves patience, persistence, and commitment, especially on the part of those helping children to engage in this process. Yust writes, "Connections between personal and faith stories require that the stories of children's lives be valued by adults and that the narratives that make up the story of the religious tradition are as accessible to children as their own stories are."[26] Drawing from Yust's interpretation of story-linking, I'll present three broad ways in which adults can help children move from story-telling and story-hearing to story-living.

Celebrations

First, pastors, teachers, and parents can help children to connect their stories to God's story through celebration.[27] I began the preceding chapter with some words about the festival of Passover. This is a perfect example of Jewish story-linking through celebration. Children are invited into the celebration to ask questions about how this festival fits into their story. They learn about how God's liberation of the Israelites thousands of years ago matters to them today.

Christians have their own festivals that, although hijacked by mass market society, can help children connect their stories to God's story. Christmas is a prime example. After all, we all come into the world just like Jesus, as a vulnerable baby. And Easter gives us the opportunity to

23. Ibid., 25.
24. Ibid., 26.
25. Ibid.
26. Yust, *Real Kids*, 42.
27. Ibid., 60.

share our resurrection stories—tales of how we've experienced new beginnings after significant losses—and help children understand how Christ's life, death, and resurrection affect how we live today.

Christian feasts and festivals aren't the only celebrations that can help children move toward story-living. The everyday events of our lives—washing our faces, brushing our teeth, making dinner, doing homework, passing out a snack—can become celebrations of God's story.[28] But it requires us to engage in what McLaren refers to as "faithing our practices."[29] We faith our practices when we connect simple aspects of our everyday lives with God's cosmic story. Brushing our teeth might become a ritual that speaks of how God scrubs us clean from our sins. Passing out a snack at Sunday school can be likened to the hospitality that Christ showed to those in need. There are countless ways in which the stories of our lives and the lives of children can be connected to God's story through faithing the practices in our day-to-day living.

SAY IT AGAIN

A second way to link our stories to God's story is through retelling the narrative of God. After children hear God's story, they can put it into their own words in order to better understand it and own it as their story. After all, "Children put stories in their own words by linking them to their own experiences or understandings of social life."[30]

Through their lived experiences and their imaginations, children can wonder about how different chapters in God's story might have unfolded, what various characters might have looked like or felt, and how they are similar to and different from these characters. In this way, God's story is appropriated into the lives, experiences, and imaginations of children. And it moves one step closer to becoming their story.

BECOMING ACTORS IN GOD'S STORY

Third, children live God's story by becoming part of the story, by seeing themselves as actors within God's epic drama. This is a crucial move from the past to the present and future, from looking at what has already happened in God's story to imagining how they can shape the narrative

---

28. Ibid., 63.
29. McLaren, *Finding Our Way*, 181.
30. Yust, *Real Kids*, 64.

in their everyday lives. This is the heart of story-living: helping God's story to unfold through our own lives.

This might mean examining themes in the Bible—peace, justice, humility, hospitality, and the stranger—and discovering how to make them come alive in the world. Since God's story involves welcoming the stranger, children can wonder about who today's strangers are and how they can welcome them. As characters in God's story listened for God's voice, young disciples can explore the many ways in which God might be speaking to them on this very day. However parents and practitioners aid children in living into God's story, it is vital that they help them see that God's story isn't over, that they are a part of the narrative, and that they can shape the future of this cosmic story.

The threefold movement of the story strategy speaks to children of all spiritual styles. It involves understanding God's story, using our emotions to connect to it, wondering about the narrative of God, and engaging in action to keep the story alive today, tomorrow, and for years to come. And although there are ways to help children of all spiritual styles engage in the story strategy, the meaning that the children make through this process will be affected by their dominant styles. It is very important that as adults we avoid stifling young people's spiritual styles or projecting our dominant styles onto children.

In *Formational Children's Ministry*, Ivy Beckwith makes three shifts in how those who work with children might think about the Bible and children. First, they can intentionally avoid over-interpreting God's story, and let the Bible speak for itself, having faith that not only will children enter the story in their own ways, but that God will speak to them through these encounters.[31] Second, they can "allow space for children to explore the story in ways that are meaningful to them."[32] And, third, they can resist their desires to tell children what the different aspects of God's story mean. They can avoid telling them what the points of the stories are.[33] When we who minister with children take Beckwith's advice, we allow young people to approach the narrative of God, walk around in

---

31. Beckwith, *Formational*, 34.
32. Ibid., 35.
33. Ibid., 37.

it, and become a part of it without checking their spiritual styles at the door.

Spiritual styles serve as lenses through which people narrate their lives, encounter God's story, and connect the two. This is a good thing! It allows children's dominant styles to come into play as they tell, hear, and live their stories. And when the story strategy is used in groups, it reminds us—young and old alike—that there are many ways to tell, hear, or live out these stories. We can use words, emotion, symbols, and action as we reflect on our lives, enter God's story, and make God's story our own. It is no wonder, then, that story is a remarkable strategy for nurturing children of all spiritual styles.

7

Ministry on the Frontlines

Tactics for Including All Children

W E HAVE SEEN IN chapters 5 and 6 that nurturing the spirituality of all children involves the intentional use of broad strategies, such as welcoming children and connecting their stories to God's story. Yet in order for these long-term, overarching strategies to produce the desired outcome of spiritual trans/formation and experiences of God, key short-term tactics must also be in place within any ministry involving children, and any ministry in general.

According to one dictionary, the word *tactics* usually refers to the "science and art of disposing and maneuvering forces in combat."[1] Another definition adds that this word can refer to "immediate or short-range plans and means adopted in carrying out a scheme or achieving some end."[2] While deploying ground, air, and naval troops would be a wider strategy aimed at producing the desired result of a military victory, these troops must be deployed according to specific tactics, like having a battalion of ground troops encroach on enemy territory, setting an ambush on advancing foes, or directing naval vessels to surround an enemy ship according to a specific tactical formation. Such "short-range" tactics, when utilized under the umbrella of larger strategies, work together to defeat the enemy, gain key information, and fulfill one's mandate.

As Christians, our mandate includes producing individuals and faith communities committed to living out the teachings of Jesus within the traditions of the church as they fulfill the command to love God

---

1. *Merriam-Webster's Collegiate Dictionary*, 11th ed., s.v., "tactics."
2. *Canadian Oxford Dictionary*, 2nd ed., s.v., "tactics."

and other people. Just as the military requires tactics in order to accomplish the goals of their mandate, faith communities need to use tactics to develop authentic children of God and disciples of Jesus Christ. We need procedures and plans in place to bring about this end. However, it is important to keep in mind that children experience God according to their dominant spiritual styles and are more apt to do so (and to feel included in churches) when the needs of these styles are nurtured within environments in which all children fit.

Craig Dykstra believes that people require practices that order and shape their lives in ways that allow their existence to have integrity and meaning.[3] Likewise, for ministries with children to be meaningful and to have integrity, they need to be shaped by specific practices, in this case, those which meet the spiritual needs of children and help them to have transcendental experiences with the almighty God.

In this chapter, I offer advice about how churches can use practices and create environments in which children of the four spiritual styles can each feel included and have their spiritual needs addressed. Keeping in mind the lives of the thirteen children from Northview Community Church, Townsend Baptist Church, and Lawrence Park Presbyterian Church, I'll outline a number of ministry methods geared towards nurturing children of each spiritual style. These tactics can help children of each specific style to experience God and feel included in their faith communities. In essence, the ideas that follow were offered to me by the children themselves, as outlined in chapter 3 and 4. My role has simply been to organize them, elaborate upon them, and bolster them through practical approaches and models of ministry with children.

While there are countless models, methods, and practices that nurture the spiritual trans/formation of children of the four spiritual styles, what I present are generalized suggestions about methods and practices which I believe to be particularly effective for nurturing the spiritual lives of young people. These aren't formulas for guaranteeing results. Although ministry models and techniques that prove to be useful in one congregation might be inappropriate or unproductive in another, I believe that these suggestions can work to create spaces of intentional inclusivity and environments of harmonious dissonance.

---

3. Dykstra, *Growing*, 7.

MORE THAN JUST TALKING HEADS: TACTICS FOR NURTURING WORD-CENTERED CHILDREN

A central concern of a word-centered style of spirituality is the illumination of the mind. Children who have a spirituality marked by this style can be nurtured through ministries that emphasize the cognitive understanding of God, the Bible, the church, and other spiritual, religious, and theological matters. Although many congregations and children's ministries already emphasize intellectual and cognitive gains in a child's understanding, this doesn't necessarily mean that they are meeting the spiritual needs of children of this style. Rather, churches must exercise a degree of intentionality as they seek to nurture children who focus on words. Drawing from the testimonies of Megan, Keira, Ben, and Nicholas, as well as the work of scholars and practitioners, let me present tactics that can help to nurture word-centered children.

At the core of a word-centered approach is the Bible—the revealed word of God. People of this spiritual style are apt to believe, along with Larry Fowler, that when children's ministry is not grounded on the Bible, it is "merely morality training."[4] Clearly, word-centered children can be included through the cognitive study of the Bible—by reading, studying, and memorizing the Christian Scriptures.[5] In order to nurture these young people, Lawrence Richards believes that the fundamental task of the teacher is to "translate the great truths of Christian faith into terms that can be both understood and experienced by boys and girls as they grow up in the Christian community."[6] From studying Scripture to making narratives come alive through skits, the cognitive abilities of the child must be stimulated through teaching and learning that helps young people increase their knowledge of the Bible and God.

Although knowledge and understanding about the Bible is important to children of this spiritual style, it mustn't be the sole purpose of teaching the Bible and using the Scriptures in children's ministry. According to the quote I just offered from Richards, children must be able to understand *and* experience the Bible within ministries and congregations. Even though some people might only be concerned with learning about the Bible, the power of Scripture need not be limited to

---

4. Fowler, *Rock-Solid*, 42.
5. Carlson and Crupper, "Instructional-Analytic," 130.
6. Richards, *Theology*, 123.

cognitive gains. In addition to being *informative*, the Bible can be *trans/formative*. In the words of Dykstra, "it is also crucial that we see the Bible as a living force and active agent, rather than as a dead relic or historic fossil, at least if we are to study and teach it correctly."[7]

Our task isn't just to help children read and understand the Bible; it is to help them see that the Bible reads them. By using the Bible as a mirror for their own lives, children can better understand themselves. The Scriptures can shape our lives and the lives of the children with whom we interact. We must allow the Scriptures to "get under our skin" and take hold of us until we let ourselves be trans/formed by them.

How are parents and practitioners supposed to help children to be read by the Bible, to be trans/formed by it? Perhaps the most important factor is that we know the children in our midst. It's not enough to only understand *our* hopes and wishes for children. We must also understand *their* perspectives, their views, hopes, troubles, and needs. This can be done through strategies like those I offered in the previous two chapters, as well as the methods for hearing children's voices that I presented in chapter 2. By welcoming children, hearing their voices, and knowing the young ones in our lives, we can help to read the Bible into the lives of children.

This is good teaching. It starts "not with teaching but with learning; and a good teacher begins not with his or her own perspective but with the learner's perspective."[8] By learning about the children in our midst, we can help them to be informed and trans/formed by the Christian Scriptures. Such a task is central to ministry with children, especially those whose spirituality is dominated by words.

What I have offered in the previous paragraphs constitute practices that reach to the very core of a style of spirituality marked by words—and of the Christian message. But these aren't the only practices or tactics that can foster spiritual trans/formation and meet the needs of children of this style. Let me offer a few more words to those who are looking for additional ways of nurturing children who focus on words.

First, allow me to speak about the content of ministry. Content matters a great deal to these children, for it establishes what is to be learned about God and faith. While the Bible can certainly be included in the content, it need not push all other topics to the sidelines. Why not teach

7. Dykstra, *Growing*, 151.
8. Ibid., 153.

children about church history, introducing them to their own faith tradition and the great saints that have come before them? Theology is another wonderful topic for children of this spiritual style, but one must be cautious to keep the material appropriate to the ages and developmental characteristics of the children. Social issues might also interest children of this style. Perhaps ministers, teachers, and parents can help young people explore how their insight into the Bible, history, and theology might inform significant world issues and events. And why not design some teaching around what the children themselves are interested in learning? In this way, children will know that their voices and opinions are respected and appreciated.

Words matter to children of this style. Therefore, we can try to ensure that the words we use in lessons, devotions, and ministries with children are precise and accurate. By doing so, we can help young disciples to develop positive and cogent understandings of material being presented. Children certainly aren't stupid. But since they are still developing their vocabularies, complex words must be unpacked and explained so that young people can grasp their meanings. If complicated or ambiguous terms and concepts are not explained, or are used too frequently, children may become confused and frustrated. When terminology is properly explained, children learn the language of the Christian faith, a skill that too few young people possess these days.[9]

Adults don't need to "dumb down" their lessons for children. After all, children are not dumb. But adults must ensure that their teaching isn't too far beyond the children's current knowledge and abilities. We who seek to help children learn do best to ensure that material is taught in ways that are suitable to the cognitive abilities of children.[10]

This brings us to the work of Lev Vygotsky, a psychologist who argued that children learn best by engaging in material that is between what they are capable of doing by themselves and what they can accomplish with the assistance and supervision of teachers, mentors, and other children. Vygotzky referred to this as the zone of proximal development, which he defined as "the distance between the actual developmental level

---

9. Smith with Denton, *Soul Searching*, 131–33.

10. Several scholars have written on teaching according to the cognitive abilities of children, one of whom is Cathy Stonehouse. See Stonehouse, *Joining Children*, 73–84. An excellent introductory volume about human development and the life of faith is Kelcourse, *Human Development*.

as determined by independent problem solving and the level of potential development as determined through problem solving under adult guidance or in collaboration with more capable peers."[11] By keeping the exercises and material of lessons with children slightly beyond their present understanding and abilities but not so far beyond that they cannot succeed without assistance or collaboration, adults can help children engage in the continual development of their minds and make gains in their knowledge of God, the Bible, and other matters of importance.

Since children of this spiritual style focus on understanding God and the Bible, many of them may ask questions during and after lessons, devotions, and programs, especially if the material engages the children in their zones of proximal development. When this happens, children may experience cognitive dissonance, an uneasy feeling brought about by contradictions in one's thinking, and they might require clarification or further instruction to achieve balanced and cohesive understanding. Adults should respectfully and graciously acknowledge questions or comments and offer clear, precise answers. If you're not able to answer a question, you can explore possible answers together with the inquisitive child. None of us know everything—especially when it comes to transcendental matters. So we may, with humility and care, join children in exploring questions and ideas to which we have no precise answers. Perhaps when adults and children put their minds together, they can achieve new and surprising insight.

Finally, congregations can provide inclusive and nurturing environments for word-centered children by ensuring that their young congregants have access to a wide range of resources at church libraries. For these children, "reading is the avenue of God's speech"[12] and reading beyond the Bible is vital to trans/formation. By accessing an ample collection of resources—at church and at home—children can satisfy their spiritual needs through reading and learning about God, the Bible, and other subjects.

Furthermore, adults should take time to read with the children to whom they minister, for through this practice, they can joyfully learn together. Even though Richard Foster refers to the practice of study as an "inward discipline,"[13] it need not occur in isolation. Through reading

11. Vygotsky, *Mind in Society*, 86.
12. Ware, *Discover*, 86.
13. Foster, *Celebration*.

with children, spirit touches spirit as the inner lives of adults and children connect to one another. As Bonnie Miller-McLemore has pointed out, "Children are a gift. Books are a gift. Engaging both can be an immense pleasure in life."[14]

MORE THAN JUST FEELING GOOD: TACTICS FOR NURTURING EMOTION-CENTERED CHILDREN

In *Children in the Worshipping Community*, David Ng and Virginia Thomas poignantly state, "Music and children are a natural combination."[15] Such a statement is particularly true for children with a spiritual style marked by emotion. These young people revel in experiences that involve connecting and communing with God through emotional music. Therefore, churches and ministries that wish to be inclusive of children with an emotion-centered approach to spirituality would miss the mark if they didn't intentionally include elements of music in their curricula, ministries, and activities.

Nurturing these children, however, is not as simple as popping a CD into a stereo and assuming that this creates an aural avenue through which these children can experience God. A degree of intentionality is required when planning to help children transcend the here and now and encounter God through music.

Choosing music that meets the needs of emotion-centered children isn't a task to be taken lightly. Music has a quality that guides one's feelings and experiences and has transcendental power beyond comprehension. Scholars and music therapists recognize that "music possesses an intrinsic expressive power that can be manifested in different ways."[16] It has the unique ability to penetrate multiple dimensions of human life—the physical, emotional, mental, and spiritual.[17] Since it is so vital to this spiritual style, let me offer a few brief suggestions for using music with children with an emotion-centered style of spirituality.

First, don't be limited by contemporary music fads. There is a richness in hymnody and traditional music that speaks to children as well as adults. When using music with children, choose a wide variety of styles,

14. Miller-McLemore, *In the Midst*, 158.
15. Ng and Thomas, *Children in the Worshipping Community*, 103.
16. Boso et al., "Neurophysiology and Neurobiology," 187.
17. Ng and Thomas, *Children in the Worshipping Community*, 103.

from medieval Gregorian chants to contemporary songs that capture the imagination through melody, harmony, instrumentation, and lyrics. Select music from the rhythmic songs of African churches to the repetitive and meditative chants of the Taizé movement. Using a wide base of music allows children to appreciate how Christians from other eras, cultures, and traditions use this universal language to worship and experience the living God. Offering children music that has enriched the church during different time periods and in different locations can help them learn early in life that there are many ways of encountering God through music.

Don Ratcliff has noted that Christians "make associations between their music and their emotions. . . . Later, although the religious experience may have been forgotten, the association between the feelings and certain music selections may remain."[18] The music that children hear at churches can have a dramatic impact on them in years to come, so it's best to expose them to a wide variety of musical styles enveloped within an environment of inclusivity and acceptance.

I've seen the impact of music on children in my wife's spiritual life. Having grown up in a German evangelical faith community, Jenny continuously yearns to hear the hymns that were sung by her childhood congregation. When we began attending a church that limited itself to contemporary Christian music, she'd sometimes feel the urge to experience God through the hymns that she heard as a child. Once in a while, she would come home from Sunday services and pull out her harmonica or sit down at the piano and play hymns like "Take My Life and Let it be" or "Come, Thou Font."

I've had similar experiences. I long to hear the wonderful songs that I heard as I grew up in the Catholic Church, songs like "City of God," and "Here I am, Lord," the latter of which my mother sang to lull me to sleep when I was very young. I remember the Sunday morning at my church in Virginia when the song leader told us to turn to hymn number six. To my joy, it was "Gather Us In," a song that I sang with my church quite often when I was high school. But I hadn't heard this song in church services for many years. Immediately, this song evoked a religious memory that gave me a deep spiritual warmth.

These experiences demonstrate that the music through which children positively experience God can impact them for years to come.

18. Ratcliff, "Music, God, and Psychology," para. 7.

Music has the transcendental power to evoke memories. How vital it is, therefore, that we allow our children to worship God through several musical styles and in an inclusive and loving environment. We wouldn't want to leave them with bad memories to trouble them for years to come.

Another point to remember about using music with children is that it's important to take the lyrical content of songs into consideration when selecting music. Although songs have the ability to evoke strong emotions, they also convey theological ideas through lyrics. Choose songs with lyrics that are simple enough to be understood by children, but espouse good theology.

When ministering with young children, be careful not to choose songs with abstract lyrics, like those that talk about how "Jesus is in my heart." Young children think in concrete manners and aren't usually able to grasp more complex and abstract ideas. I remember hearing that Jesus was in my heart when I was a young tyke. Without the cognitive ability to engage in abstract thought, I figured that I had a part of Jesus in my actual heart—maybe his pinky toe or his earlobe. I wondered what parts of Jesus were in my parents' hearts and how Jesus' body parts were distributed to so many people. Furthermore, children might struggle to understand some words that appear in Christian music, like "Hallelujah," "praise," "Gloria," and "Hosanna." It is helpful to explain what these words mean and why they are included in songs. When examining lyrics, don't forget to take into account the cognitive abilities of the children in your ministries.

My wife and I know from experience that finding songs that are appropriate for the musical and cognitive abilities children yet are also theologically rich is no lean feat. When we prepare to lead music with children, we sometimes find ourselves struggling to select songs that are theologically rich, yet lyrically simple. We can easily find many theologically-shallow songs with simple lyrics, and several songs that espouse a rich theology through complex words. We kept searching, and over time we discovered songs that are rich in theology, yet relatively simple in their lyrics. A roster of such wonderful songs might include "All Creatures of Our God and King," "Down to the River to Pray," "Not Forgotten," "Were You There?," "Let There be Peace on Earth," "I Love You, Lord," and "Here I Am, Lord."

Let me offer a few more tips for selecting music that is appropriate for children, especially those who are very young. Use songs with repeated phrases so that children can rely on their memory rather than reading or vocabulary skills.[19] By doing so, you can help children to focus on singing to God, rather than paying too much attention to trying to read a lot of words on a projection screen or the pages of a hymnal. It's also helpful to choose songs that are easy to sing and are free of complex rhythms and melodies,[20] for many children are still developing their singing capabilities. Using songs that are too far beyond their abilities could cause them to feel frustrated and could hinder them from experiencing the Almighty. And don't forget about the remarkable power of instrumental music, a language that goes beyond words.

Although it can be difficult to choose songs that meet all of these conditions, it's wise to critically examine the music used with children to ensure that at least some of these suggestions are taken. If children might not understand all the lyrics of a song, explain what the words mean and use it as an opportunity for teaching. If you're not sure about a song, try it out and see what happens. Maybe it will end up being a keeper! Just be careful not to introduce too many new songs to children at one time. Bombarding them with a lot of new songs at once can close children off to the music and the connection with God. And don't worry about making sure that every song you use with children meets all of the above guidelines. Having some songs that are easy to sing, others that espouse rich and accurate theology, and still others that originated in different cultures can work together to provide a wonderful musical environment for children with an emotion-centered approach to spirituality.

To adequately nurture the emotional spirituality of children of this style, churches must offer opportunities for children to participate in authentic worship, especially musical worship. Marva Dawn reminds us that "because worship is, usually quite subtly, a strong formative agent, we must be sure that what we do in worship nurtures the kind of people we want our children and ourselves to be as Church."[21] As participants in worship, children can be involved in formal congregational worship and informal, small-group worship, the latter of which "reveals inner spiri-

19. Ng and Thomas, *Children in the Worshipping Community*, 106.

20. Hopkins, "How to Lead Music," 116.

21. Dawn, *Is it a Lost Cause?* 66.

tual lives to both children and adults"[22] in more intimate and personal settings.

Including children in worship allows them to engage with others in singing praises to God and to understand that they are not alone as they do so. Through corporate musical worship, children can see that they are a part of something greater than they are; they're a part of a great cloud of witnesses that spans across time and space and joins creation in singing praises to God.[23] Through engaging in musical worship as a community, "an embodied theology—a way of living and thinking about life in relationship to God—is formed and expressed."[24] Such tactics help children to be trans/formed into members of faith communities who seek to authentically experience God and show God's love to the world.

Remember also that while music may be a more powerful and popular means of evoking emotional connections to God, it's definitely not the only means. Drama and dance are other ways in which children can be trans/formed by feeling God's presence, especially children who are kinesthetic learners or seem to be in states of perpetual motion. Why not organize a drama or dance program at your congregation and allow the children involved in it to perform for their friends and family members or, even better, the entire congregation? But, as with music, be sure that the styles of dance and the topics of the dramatic presentations are suitable for the children and espouse theology and values that are appropriate for your faith tradition and context.

A word of warning before moving on to the next spiritual style: guard yourself from evoking emotions for the sake of evoking emotions. Being emotional is not actually what matters most for children of this style. What matters is that emotional experiences allow them to feel the presence of God. Don't simply select pieces of music or dramatic presentations because they are emotionally-charged. Doing so exploits children's emotional sensitivity and undercuts the goals of an emotion-centered spirituality. In all you do, make it authentic and centered on God.

---

22. Allen, "Nurturing Children's Spirituality in Intergenerational," 269.

23. Saliers, "Singing Our Lives," 184.

24. Ibid., 193.

MORE THAN JUST SILENCE: TACTICS FOR NURTURING
SYMBOL-CENTERED CHILDREN

One way that inclusivity with symbol-centered children can be fostered is through intentional times and spaces for prayer. Prayer can take many forms, so children should be free to pray in diverse ways, rather than being limited to "fold your hands, close your eyes, and repeat after me." Children can be given opportunities to lead prayers in manners they prefer, including quiet, inner prayer, centering prayer, breath prayers (short, one-line prayers repeated during long, soothing breaths), or call-and-response prayers.

During a particular weekend program, I used privacy screens to convert a corner of the room into a "prayer corner." I placed a rug on the floor with fluffy pillows and stuffed sheep as reminders of Jesus, the Good Shepherd. This provided children with a place to get away from the noise and crowd of the other children and spend some time in quiet prayer with God. A few of the young people at this program were particularly drawn to the prayer corner each session and seemed to need that time alone with God in order to participate in other group activities. When I looked over to the corner, I saw children kneeling, bowing their heads, holding stuffed sheep, and whispering prayers to God. When children are given opportunities to engage in authentic prayer, mystics will be more apt to experience God within their congregation's ministries.

Out of the thirteen children in the focus groups, Caleb, Laurie, Freddy, and Ian—those with a symbol-centered spirituality—seemed to be most significantly affected by the physical environments of their churches. Unfortunately, they were also the most likely to be negatively affected by these spaces. They felt crowded and closed in, like they were being "crammed inside of a locker," to borrow Laurie's words. This reminds practitioners and parents to provide spacious areas for children, especially outdoors. Perhaps, should the weather allow for it, ministries can be held outside, where children experience God's vast creation first-hand.

Symbol-centered children tend to feel safest and closest to God in places that are outside and among God's creation, so if adults want to evoke positive experiences and memories in these children, a simple first step is to go outdoors. Perhaps nature walks can become a regular or semi-regular part of ministries. Throughout the year, adults can lead young people on these walks and then guide them in a response activity like drawing pictures of what they saw among God's creation. At the end of the year, they would have created a library of images documenting the changing of the seasons.

Congregations can create peace gardens with various types of plants. Adults and children can work together to plant and care for these gardens and the whole community can benefit from the serenity and aromas that they might sense from them. Including vegetables in some gardens can help children to understand where their food comes from and tending to the garden can be used as a teaching tool to remind children of the vulnerability and fragility of the natural world. Through gardening with children, faith communities can not only satisfy young people's desire to be in and among God's natural world; it can also help children to learn about creation care. Now more than ever, such learning is crucial.

Allowing symbol-centered children time out-of-doors can also satisfy their desire to encounter God through nature, a need that cannot be met in a classroom or gymnasium. And it can counteract what Richard Louv calls "nature-deficit disorder," a lack of exposure to the natural world, which he argues results in a number of behavior disorders. Perhaps this explains why Ian, the only child with a behavior disorder, moved everyone out of the church building during the social mapping exercise. Maybe he felt a lot like Louv: "The trees were my Ritalin. Nature calmed me, focused me, and yet excited my senses."[25]

Children of this spiritual style can be provided with worship and ministries that transform everyday times and spaces into those that are sacred and infused with holiness.[26] This can be accomplished through quiet, a slow pace, and wonder. Although often overlooked, quiet is a legitimate spiritual practice through which people can connect to God, for as Thomas à Kempis wrote many years ago, "In the silence and quietness of heart a devout soul profiteth much ... that she may be so much the more familiar with God."[27] Dallas Willard goes so far as to say that only through practices of silence and contemplation can individuals and communities experience "life-transforming concentration upon God."[28]

25. Louv, *Last Child*, 10.
26. Stewart and Berryman, *Young Children*, 13.
27. Thomas à Kempis, *Imitation*, 41.
28. Willard, *Spirit*, 164.

Another tactic for nurturing children with a symbol-centered spirituality has to do with the pace of ministries. These young people tend to experience God in calm and peaceful environments. Thus, the pace of ministries should be slow, not rushing the children, but allowing time for reflection.[29] Ministries without a slow, calm rhythm put children in danger of passing by "great things without ever being able to grasp, interiorize, and make these realities [their] own."[30] Although a flashy, fast-paced ministry may entertain young people, it can do so to the detriment of mystics. This doesn't mean, however, that the entirety of a ministry or program must be slow and calm. It's certainly appropriate to engage children in activities involving movement and energy, like dance. But without opportunities to encounter God in slow, calm, and reflective ways, children with a symbol-centered spirituality are at risk of being left behind.

Overall, ministries that meet the needs of this spiritual style focus on God with mystery, wonder, reverence, and awe. Rather than giving answers, adults can wonder together with children, for when adults wonder, it allows the children time and space to do likewise.[31] This ministry style respects the thoughtfulness of children and avoids presenting a "kiddie Gospel" that focuses on token answers and moralisms.[32] It allows the self to have spirit-to-Spirit connections to the God of wonders.

In order to create appropriate spaces for mystery and wonder, churches may include symbols and rituals in their ministries. These aspects of ministry allow children to reflect on that which is transcendent and they "help provide formational stability and familiarity."[33] Symbols speak to the human spirit in ways that words can never do and they have an incredible trans/formative power. It's in the best interest of symbol-centered children that the adults in their lives—whether pastors or parents—surround them with the great and timeless symbols of the church. I remember constantly looking around my church as a child and studying the details in the statues, the eternal flame, seasonal banners,

29. May, "Contemplative-Reflective," 70.

30. Cavalletti, *Religious Potential*, 60.

31. Berryman, *Godly Play*, 62.

32. The term "kiddie Gospel" was coined by Gretchen Wolff Pritchard in *Offering the Gospel to Children*.

33. May, "Contemplative-Reflective," 63.

and stained-glass windows. An environment saturated by symbolism was formative for my spiritual life.

Rituals involve symbolic movements that, when performed over and over again with others in a community of practice, take on trans/formative meaning.[34] Rituals like foot washing, the passing of the peace, and candle lighting can help children to connect with God, feel as though they fit in the faith community, and shape their identities as members of their communities of practice. I can attest first-hand to the formative power of rituals and symbols in the lives of children. As I disclosed in the introduction, the symbols and rituals that I witnessed in church as a child compelled me to stay in the sanctuary with my family rather than heading to children's liturgy. And they formed me early on to be a person who values and appreciates symbols and rituals for their ability to connect me to God.

When all these characteristics—quiet times and spaces, the natural world, open areas, a slow pace, wonder, symbols, and rituals—are present, an intentional environment that nurtures this spiritual style can be created.[35] Such an environment maximizes the potential for children to become creatively engaged, experience God, and have meaningful insight.[36] It allows them to be included in their faith communities and sense the transcendental presence of the God of wonder.

MORE THAN JUST GETTING THINGS DONE: TACTICS FOR NURTURING ACTION-CENTERED CHILDREN

Browsing through the prepackaged, marketed curricula available from Christian bookstores and publishers, it appears as though few (if any) are geared toward satisfying the spiritual needs of children with an action-centered approach to spirituality. In *Making Your Children's Ministry the Best Hour of Every Kid's Week*, Sue Miller and David Staal make it clear that, when it comes to the education and trans/formation of children, "application-oriented teaching is important."[37] And they're right! But for children whose spiritual style is dominated by action, the "application-oriented teaching" of many mass-marketed curricula too

34. Beckwith, *Formational*, 70–71.

35. An excellent resource for practitioners who would like to incorporate aspects of this ministry style is Berryman, *Teaching Godly Play*.

36. Stonehouse, "Knowing God," 38.

37. Miller and Staal, *Making Your Children's Ministry*, 72.

often focuses on individual choices and personal morals and fails to nurture the world-changing drive of these children. They need more than reminders to share their lunches—they need to meet children who don't have lunches; they need to organize food drives, go on fasts, and fight for justice in the lives of those who live in situations marked by injustice.

The lack of prepackaged resources for action-centered children isn't an excuse to overlook these young disciples. Prayer, as demonstrated by Juliet, the ten-year-old action-centered child from Lawrence Park Presbyterian Church, is vital to this style. The suggestions surrounding prayer that I outlined while discussing ministry with mystic children can also be applied here. But prayer with children of this spiritual style goes beyond requesting that God grants them a good day and thanking the Lord for pets. Some prayer must be intentionally dedicated to asking God to alleviate the suffering of the oppressed, marginalized, and poor, as well as soliciting God's help in changing the world. And, of course, prayer with these children can focus on partnering with what God is already doing to bring about justice across the globe.

Children can be agents of change; "their dependence on love and care keeps them open to an ever new and surprising future,"[38] one in which they are able to make a difference. Although often unnoticed, the achievements of young people can be seen around the world.[39] In Canada, for example, Craig Kielburger began an organization to fight child labor and promote education when he was only twelve years old! Speaking from experience, he writes, "At first, no one believed that children could actually make a difference. But they can. We proved it."[40] He and his brother Marc have written resources for children and young people seeking to make a difference in the world. One of their books, *Take Action! A Guide to Active Citizenship*, may be useful to parents and pastors seeking to appropriately guide their children's action-centered spirituality. In addition, Free the Children offers free curricula and resources on their website[41] that are "designed to give students a comprehensive, critical understanding of global social justice issues. . . . It starts

---

38. Herzog, *Children and Our Global Future*, 165.

39. Ibid., 164.

40. Kielburger and Kielburger, *Take Action*, vi.

41. http://www.freethechildren.com.

in the class but reaches far beyond by empowering young students to take action for positive change."[42]

One way for congregations to nurture children of this style is to provide them with opportunities to make decisions, promote change, and help those in need within their own communities and around the world. Although they, like adults, might make mistakes (who doesn't?), pastors, teachers, and parents can risk giving children the power to make decisions and get things done.[43] Juliet's church, for example, encourages her to work alongside others at their barbeques for the homeless and to participate in Operation Christmas Child's shoe box campaign.[44] With regard to the content of ministries, this spiritual style can be nurtured by encouraging "a sense of connectedness to develop tolerance, empathy and compassion."[45] Furthermore, ministries can work to teach children about the world's social injustices as a way of empowering them to make a difference.

Too often, adults seek to protect children from hearing about the evils in the world for fear that they may become afraid or depressed. Doing so, however, can rob children of the capacity to think critically and deal with experiences in their particular social locations.[46] It can also lead to "mean-world syndrome,"[47] a fear of what one doesn't know or understand in the world. It's true that children might become frustrated or upset when they hear about injustice in the world. But Marc Kielburger recommends that children turn their anger and frustration into action.[48] Such an attitude allowed him and his brother to free chil-

42. Free the Children, "FTC Curriculum."

43. Herzog, *Children and Our Global Future*, 166.

44. Studies have shown that children such as Juliet, who are involved in their local congregations in such ways, are likely to care about issues of social justice and responsibility, have a sense of being cared for by those in the community, and have positive relationships with adults. See Roehlkepartain and Patel, "Congregations," 326.

45. de Souza, "Educating for Hope," 173.

46. Erricker, "Against the Protection," 5.

47. Mean-world syndrome is a theory posited by George Gerbner that argues that a child's increasing awareness of violence and destruction through television and films "results in a reduced sensitivity to the consequences of violence along with an increased sense of vulnerability and dependence" (Gerbner, "Reclaiming," para. 9). I believe that intentionally discussing violence and social evils and examining ways to alleviate such problems can positively result in the ability to think critically about violence in the media, rather than becoming fearful of a world that is perceived as mean and dangerous.

48. Kielburger and Kielburger, *Take Action*, viii.

dren from socially constructed conceptions that say they must be seen and not heard and that they are too young to make a difference.[49]

In *The Danger of Raising Nice Kids*, Tim Smith writes the following words about parenting, which I believe speak volumes about ministry with action-centered children:

> The goal of effective parenting [and ministry with children] is not to raise safe, nice kids. It's to raise strong ones. Living a purposeful and influential life requires taking risks—lots and lots of calculated daily risks. But the risks can be processed within the context of a well-guarded harbor. That's what our homes [and congregations] can represent to our children. The fact is, home is where life is making up its mind. Therefore our homes [and congregations] must provide the kind of framework that encourages children to make some of the most dangerous decisions in their life. It's where they need to decide what their mission in life is going to be, who their mate is going to be and, most important, who their master is going to be.[50]

Instead of sheltering young people from injustices in the world and overprotecting them, faith communities can teach children about God's desire for them to bring about changes for the betterment of the global community. They can provide children and families with opportunities to connect with the poor and oppressed in personal ways and at levels of deepening intensity. We need to let young people of this spiritual style see the tears in the eyes of the poor, oppressed, and marginalized. In an article I wrote with Brian McLaren, Dan Jennings, and Karen-Marie Yust, we offer the following suggestion:

> A suburban preschool child might begin with her family sponsoring a child in Africa. In her elementary years, she might experience a summer exchange program with Native American children, leading to an inner-city immersion in middle school, followed by spending a summer among the urban poor in high school. Or a family might affiliate with a single helping organization, such as Habitat for Humanity, and involve their children first in limited contact activities (fund-raising, food contributions), then at a moderate level (landscaping and words of sup-

49. Kielburger, "Free the Children," 98–99.

50. Smith, *Danger of Raising*, 7.

port), and finally in full engagement (building alongside family members).[51]

Connecting with the oppressed and downtrodden first-hand was incredibly meaningful to Juliet. When her church provided her with the opportunity to come face-to-face with the homeless during their downtown barbeque lunch, she saw the tears in the eyes of the less fortunate. This personal connection added fuel to her fire for justice. She wanted to do more than simply send a shoe box of supplies to poor children in other parts of the world. It boosted her desire to connect with those who are less fortunate, to hear their stories, and to help them first-hand. Through personal encounters with the poor, oppressed, and marginalized that are appropriate for the ages and experiences of children, young pilgrims with an action-centered spirituality can be nurtured and encouraged along the spiritual journey to stamp out injustice.

This can be dangerous, risky work. But it can also be incredibly meaningful to people with an action-centered approach to spirituality. If we help children to encounter those suffering from injustice and enter their worlds in relative safety, we can all become one with them in solidarity against poverty, racism, discrimination, and exploitation. As Paulo Freire has written, "Solidarity requires that one enter into the situation of those with whom one is solidary."[52]

I don't encourage parents and practitioners to put children in harm's way just for the sake of doing so. But I do believe that we who raise and work with children can sometimes be overprotective because of our own fears. We need to look our fears in the eyes and see that maybe we don't have to be so afraid after all.

I remember being fearful when I visited the ghettos and housing projects on my trips to an impoverished area of eastern North Carolina. But in the midst of this fear, as I saw the terrible living conditions and the extinguished hope in the lives of the people living there, my desire for justice came into full bloom. My fear turned to anger and my anger turned to action. Through these first-hand encounters with abject poverty and social injustice on the streets of Mount Olive and Goldsboro, I discovered that James Cone is absolutely right: "Christ is in the ghetto,"[53]

51. Csinos et al., "Where are the Children?" 19.

52. Freire, *Pedagogy of the Oppressed*, 49.

53. Cone, *Black Theology*, 66.

working to stir up hope and justice amidst the community. Let us face our fears in our call to raise children who are aware that life isn't always fair, that bad things happen to good people, and that injustice has no place in God's kingdom.

When helping children learn about injustice and get to know those who are oppressed, it is important to be cautious not to do too much too soon. Ministry with action-centered children can involve a gradual process of learning and resisting injustice that is appropriate for children's development at different ages. Start small, by sponsoring a child or collecting food for your local food bank. But don't stay small. Vygotsky reminded us earlier in this chapter that children (and adults) grow when they extend slightly beyond their comfort zones and what they are capable of doing themselves.[54]

Let me offer a final word of caution. Remember that changing the structures of injustice in our world is difficult work. It's important that we openly discuss this with children. Many action-centered individuals never see the results of their efforts. It is impossible for any one person to break down walls that separate human beings from one another and hinder them from living full lives. Often, all that action-centered people can do is chip away at injustice one piece at a time. Pastors, parents, and teachers need to be sure that they are not setting up action-centered children to feel overwhelmed and disappointed when these young activists don't see the full results of their labor. Keep your goals realistic and be sure to be make it clear to children that while their work is extremely important, it is a small part of a great struggle. But as many individuals work to chip away at injustice in their own corners of the globe, the systems, ideologies, and people that keep human beings in oppression will gradually be broken down. "We can do no great things, only small things with great love."[55]

This is the role of congregations in nurturing action-centered children: to appropriately teach, encourage, and equip them to work for justice, to join those who are oppressed and marginalized in their quests for justice, and to always remind them that they can make a difference—even if they don't see it. People of this style agree with Dr. Martin Luther King Jr., that "Injustice anywhere is a threat to justice everywhere. We are caught in an inescapable network of mutuality, tied in a single gar-

54. Vygotsky, *Mind in Society*, 86.
55. Origin uncertain; sometimes attributed to Mother Teresa of Calcutta.

ment of destiny. Whatever affects one directly, affects all indirectly."[56] The spiritual trans/formation of action-centered children involves education and practice in seeing injustice and partnering with God in the healing of our broken world.

I have recently been inspired by Gordon Ramsay to take up cooking. I had always assumed that preparing fine meals was incredibly complicated and involved many specialized ingredients. But what I've learned from flipping through Chef Ramsay's cookbooks and watching *The F Word*, *Hell's Kitchen*, and *Kitchen Nightmares*, is that sometimes the best food is also the simplest. It only takes a few ingredients to create a succulent lamb wellington or the perfect asparagus risotto. And sometimes the few ingredients needed for a dish complement one another through their differences. Honey alone can be too sweet for some dishes. So chefs mix in zesty mustard to contrast the sweetness of the honey and provide a more balanced flavor. The two simple yet contrasting ingredients work together to create harmonious dissonance—and the perfect taste.

So it is with tactics for creating environments that nurture the spiritual lives of all children: sometimes the simplest approaches are also the most effective. Why purchase expensive curricula to create action-packed, fast-paced, MTV-like programs for children, when going on a nature walk, singing simple yet meaningful hymns, or using one's imagination to enter God's story work just as well—or even better?

And, like the combination of mustard and honey, some of the best ministries and spiritual environments include contrasting elements of each spiritual style blended together in harmonious dissonance. Emotion alone can't connect all children to God in meaningful ways. But when emotion is balanced with words, action, and symbols, children are invited to experience God according to their dominant spiritual styles. This is an environment of harmony. But they are also challenged and stretched to go beyond their own style and explore ways in which other children feel the presence of the living God. This is an environment of dissonance. In fine dining and in children's ministry, less is more and contrasting flavors lead to fantastic results. And since we all have to start

56. King, "Letter," 290.

somewhere, I offer an appendix to this book with an assortment of ideas for beginning to nurture children of each style.

In this chapter, I offer advice to those seeking to nurture the spirituality of all children by presenting a number of ideas and ministry models that teachers, pastors, and parents can examine and evaluate based on the needs of their children and congregations. No single model or practice can be inclusive of children of all spiritual styles, but when aspects of each work conjunctively, every child who is present can feel a sense of inclusivity and fit within a balanced spiritual environment that welcomes and nurtures all children.

It is also crucial for adults to include elements of many of the tactics I presented so that young people don't become so embedded in their dominant style that they fall into one of its extreme forms. If such a balanced tension exists, children will be more likely to develop what Urban T. Holmes refers to as a sensible and sensitive spirituality: "'Sensibility' defines for us that sensitivity to the ambiguity of styles of prayer [and spirituality] and the possibilities for a creative dialogue within the person and within the community as it seeks to understand the experience of God and its meaning for our world."[57] Such balanced sensitivity is a mark of churches that provide all children with a healthy sense of inclusivity and fit. Through our differences, we are all made stronger.

57. Holmes, *History*, 5.

8

Looking Back, Looking Ahead
Concluding Reflections

CARL JUNG ONCE WROTE, "The shoe that fits one person pinches another; there is no recipe for living that suits all cases."[1] This is true for the spiritual lives of children—each young person expresses different manners through which they come to know and experience God. Yet within this diversity, four legitimate spiritual avenues have been demonstrated through the thirteen children who shared their experiences with me: the path of the intellect, the way of feelings, the journey of mystery, and the road to justice.

As I reflect on what I have discovered about the phenomenon of children's spirituality, I can't help but feel a sense of amazement, astonishment, and delight. I am amazed by the spiritual wisdom professed from the mouths of these thirteen children.[2] I'm astonished by their personal experiences of transcendence. And I am delighted by the spiritual diversity that God has given to even the youngest of children.

Through reflecting on my expedition into the spiritual lives of children, I have realized that this book isn't the end of the journey; it is a starting point. It's a chance for researchers to seriously consider spiritual styles and children. While there is a growing body of research into the spiritual life of children, little has been said about different styles or types of spirituality. Scholars have demonstrated the importance of narrative, wonder, worship, music, and many other practices that can nurture the life of children, but there has been no discussion about how these vital

1. Jung, *Modern Man*, 60.
2. See Ps 8:2.

practices can impact children with different styles of spirituality. It is becoming widely known in academic circles that children should be included in the life of the church, but there are very few studies that demonstrate how this can be done in manners that are inclusive of children from all styles. While this book begins to address some questions about spiritual styles, it also raises a number of questions that can only be answered with further research.

This book is also a starting point for practitioners—those on the frontlines of ministry with children. It's an invitation for churches and ministers to begin including children of all four styles, so that all young people are welcome and feel a satisfactory sense of fit within their congregations. This is of the utmost importance, for George Barna reminds us that "unless their spiritual life is prioritized and nurtured, [children] will miss out on much of the meaning, purpose and joy of life."[3] Children who don't feel included in their churches risk becoming numb to their spiritual needs and they can lose the spiritual vitality that is necessary for a healthy worldview that can sustain them through the trials of life.[4]

A PIVOTAL MOMENT

The church in North America (along with North American society) stands at a pivotal moment. Many people can sense that things are changing and that we in the church are at the cusp of something new. The dominant spiritual style of our society—an emotion-centered approach—is giving way. But I'm not sure which style will take its place. I can see aspects of spirituality marked by words, symbols, and action gaining ground and becoming influential in the lives of young people across the continent.

A stress on words has become evident through the growing size of congregations that emphasize a "thoughtful faith." One of these churches is The Meeting House, a large faith community based in the Greater Toronto Area. Such congregations don't shy away from providing people with thought-provoking and somewhat complex sermons that may interpret biblical books or examine Christianity through philosophy or pop culture. Rather than encouraging congregants to think certain things in certain ways, churches like The Meeting House engage people

3. Barna, *Transforming Children*, 29.
4. Bellous, *Educating Faith*, 21, 26.

in theological investigation and reflection in order to help them wrestle with difficult theological issues and develop a faith that is thoughtful and critical. And this "church for people who aren't into church" seems to strike a chord with the 5000 people who attend Sunday services, the 1200 who show up for one of many home churches, and countless more who download sermons and teachings from The Meeting House's website.[5]

To encourage people to think critically about issues of spirituality and faith, many congregations and leaders emphasize the spoken word. As one such person, Joyce Bellous stresses the importance of good preaching as she mentors, teaches, and consults with pastors and lay leaders from around the globe. The work of such congregations and individuals could be symptoms of a resurgence of a word-centered approach to spirituality across North America.

Symbol-centered tendencies seem to be rising through emerging leaders and thinkers such as Rob Bell, Peter Rollins, Tony Jones, and Brian McLaren, whose writings leave room for wondering about the mysteries of God and the phenomenon of human spirituality.

Bell's 2006 "Everything is Spiritual" tour, in which he spoke to audiences in twenty five cities about the implications of innate human spirituality, demonstrates a growth in a spirituality centered on symbolism. In his message, which became available on DVD the following year, he said, "The issue is not whether you're a spiritual being or you have a spirituality; the issue is whether your eyes are open and you're aware of it."[6]

The very title of Rollins's first book, *How (not) to Speak of God*, denotes the symbol-centered approach he takes to spirituality and faith. In this book, he says that "God is not a theoretical problem to somehow resolve but rather a mystery to be participated in."[7] Toward the beginning of his second book, *The Fidelity of Betrayal*, this philosopher/theologian reminds us that "The fragile flame of faith is fanned into life so simply: all we need to do is sit still for a few moments, embrace the silence that engulfs us, and invite that flame to burn bright within us."[8] Clearly, Rollins expresses a mystical, symbol-centered approach to spirituality— and he encourages others to do likewise.

5. http://www.themeetinghouse.ca.
6. Bell, *Everything is Spiritual*.
7. Rollins, *How (not) to Speak*, 23.
8. Rollins, *Fidelity*, 9.

As a leader in the emerging movement, Jones has taken it upon himself to reflect on how to appropriately use contemplative models of spiritual trans/formation, particularly in youth ministry. Simply from browsing through the tables of contents of some of his books, one can see that he advocates for the use of ancient practices such as centering prayer, silence and solitude, meditation, and iconography.[9]

In one of his more recent books, *Finding Our Way Again*, McLaren encourages readers to seek out an "everyday spirituality" that draws together the sacred and secular worlds. In his opinion, the emerging postmodern era "can be best characterized by a search for *spirituality*, a word that somehow captures this idea of a viable, sustainable, meaningful way of life."[10] In the manner of a true mystic, he encourages people to be more concerned with the journey than with the destination.

Bell, Rollins, Jones, and McLaren each have extensive followings and sell numerous copies of their books and resources. At their speaking engagements, they often find themselves in packed auditoriums speaking to sold-out crowds. Perhaps, through the influence of people like them, North America will move toward a symbol-centered approach to spirituality.

Finally, an action-centered spirituality might be overwhelming younger generations of North Americans—both inside and outside of the body of Christ. Social responsibility, service learning, and global citizenship seem to be on the rise among younger generations. Even though young people can be self-focused, they don't tend to be selfish and they value being considerate of others.[11]

Universities and colleges are beginning to host conferences for students concerned with issues of global poverty, violence, and injustice. My alma mater, Wilfrid Laurier University, is one such institution. Its student-led Global Citizenship Conference[12] has attracted thousands of young people to hear notable figures such as Stephen Lewis, former United Nations special envoy for HIV/AIDS in Africa, and Lieutenant-

---

9. See Jones, *Soul Shaper* and Jones, *Sacred Way*.

10. McLaren, *Finding Our Way*, 4. In this book, McLaren advocates for a balance between contemplative symbol-centered practices and justice-seeking action-centered practices. Perhaps it demonstrates a rise in both of these styles.

11. Arnett, "Suffering," 27.

12. See http://www.gcclaurier.org.

General Roméo Dallaire, the former Force Commander of the United Nations Assistance Mission for Rwanda (UNAMIR).

High school students are also developing action-centered visions. In 2008, I attended a fund-raising event that was initiated, organized, and hosted by Student Reach,[13] an organization committed to combating child poverty and was founded and directed by a group of local high school students. As I sat in the auditorium, I saw hundreds of teenagers who were intently listening to Craig Kielburger, founder of Free the Children, who told them that they can make a difference in the world.

Since 2007, Free the Children has hosted an annual event called We Day. This one-day event held in Montréal, Toronto, and Vancouver includes concerts, presentations, and speeches by notable individuals and groups like Al Gore, Jane Goodall, the fourteenth Dalai Lama, K'Naan, and Barenaked Ladies. To date, over 50,000 students from across Canada have rallied together in support of We Day, an event that kicks off "an innovative year-long program created to celebrate the power of young people to create positive change in the world."[14]

These events might foretell of a rise in a spirituality marked by action, especially among the younger generations. Will the church step up and help to bring about the goals and visions of these young people? Only time will tell.

HARMONIOUSLY DISSONANT COMMUNITIES

My hope is that none of the three previous possibilities come into full fruition. Instead, I have a dream that faith communities will follow the example of congregations like Lawrence Park Presbyterian Church, a church that offers something for every child. Whether their spiritual life is marked by words, emotion, symbols, or action, this faith community can nurture and challenge children (and all people present) towards growth.

And Lawrence Park is certainly not alone in creating a holistic environment that nurtures all styles in a balanced tension. Whether they know it or not, many churches across the continent are creating spaces for all spiritual styles. While living in Virginia, I visited one of these faith communities on a number of occasions.

13. See http://www.student-reach.com.
14. Free the Children, "2010 We Day: About the Day."

Every few months or so, my wife and I would wake up a little earlier than normal on Sunday and make the drive up I-95 and around the
Capital Beltway until we reached Spencerville, Maryland, a small town
in the Baltimore-Washington corridor. Here, we would take in the multi-
faceted services of Cedar Ridge Community Church. Under the leadership of its founder, Brian McLaren, and its current pastor, Matthew Dyer,
this community of faith has created an environment characterized by a
balanced tension of the four spiritual styles.

For word-centered people, the services at Cedar Ridge include sermons and resources that are well-researched, thought-provoking, and
based on the Christian Scriptures. For those with an emotion-centered
spirituality, its musical worship includes songs that touch the soul and
espouse appropriate theology for its context. People with a spiritual life
marked by symbols will value Cedar Ridge's candle station, where people
can offer prayers for loved ones, its "prayer walls" on which people can
express their prayers through images and words, and its openness to
having congregants sit in silent contemplation if they choose to do so.
Action-centered individuals will be drawn to its message of peace and
justice and its commitment to challenging and changing the world at
both local and global levels. They believe, in the words of their founder,
that "Everything Must Change."[15]

A key manner in which Cedar Ridge has been able to create a holistic and balanced environment is through its response time. After the
sermon and a time of musical worship, the church offers a number of
ways in which the community can choose to respond to what they just
experienced and heard. I have already mentioned the candle-lighting
station and the prayer wall. In addition, people are invited to give and
receive communion from one another at tables throughout the sanctuary; they can approach the worship band and become lost in their
music; and they can engage in conversation with one another about the
message they just heard. This is a congregation that knows the value of
harmonious dissonance.

And perhaps the best thing about Cedar Ridge is that this faith
community has begun to intentionally ask how they can better include
children in their congregational life and nurture them along the spiritual

---

15. McLaren, *Everything Must Change*.

journey. They are opening themselves to receiving the gifts that children bring to their community of faith.[16]

We in North America stand at a crossroads, unsure of the direction that the mass of our congregations will take us. Will we follow the path of words and reexamine how we can know and experience God through the illumination of the mind? Perhaps we will traverse the road of action and take up the causes of the oppressed, downtrodden, and poor. Maybe we will walk along the symbol-centered trail, wondering together about the great mysteries of the almighty God. Maybe we'll maintain a focus on how God touches our innermost being through emotion. Whatever direction the church takes, one thing is certain: without a balanced tension of the four spiritual styles, we risk falling into an aberration, or extreme form of one style and leaving behind those people who walk along different paths. In order to avoid such a sad situation, churches must engage in practices that can nurture people—especially children—from each and every spiritual style. We can transform our congregations into places of harmonious dissonance.

Bellous has written that "children's well-being indicates a society's overall health."[17] A church that fails to nurture the spirituality of all of its children is not a spiritually healthy congregation, regardless of its dominant style. But including children with spiritual lives marked by words, emotion, symbols, and action can be difficult and time-consuming. George Barna is correct in saying that "effective ministry to children—by parents or church-related youth workers—demands substantial energy, time and interaction."[18] Yet the yield from such work is well worth the effort.

Although I offer ideas about how pastors, parents, and teachers can create environments that nurture children of all spiritual styles, I know that further implications and reflections are needed. This, however, is advice that I cannot offer. Since each church, minister, parent, child, and environment is unique, a congregation's ministries must be

16. In the fall of 2008, Matthew Dyer and his pastoral team led a sermon series entitled "Roots to Branches." Through this series and a number of different projects (covering the foyer with pictures of church members as children and guiding conversations about how to include children in the faith community), Cedar Ridge has taken seriously Jesus' mandate to welcome children. To hear the "Roots to Branches" sermons, visit http://www.crcc.org/messages/series/roots-branches.

17. Bellous, *Educating Faith*, 10.

18. Barna, *Transforming Children*, 129.

individually tailored to effectively include every child. But this difficult work is imperative to the spiritual flourishing of children. Only when an environment is created that nurtures and speaks to the inquisitiveness of a word-centered spirituality, the affective nature of an emotion-centered spirituality, the wonder and mystery of a symbol-centered spirituality, and the quest for justice of an action-centered spirituality, can a church honestly say that it's including all children. But fostering an environment like this, one that is simultaneously nurturing and challenging, is possible.

MANY TREES, ONE SOIL

My father-in-law recently told me about a short trip he took one Thanksgiving weekend. As he and my mother-in-law drove up Highway 3 along the shore of Lake Erie in rural southern Ontario, he couldn't help but notice the magnificent diversity of the forests around him. Within the same forest, there were deciduous and coniferous trees, freshly-sprouted pines and old maples that might not survive the winter, trees full of leaves and some that were bare, and trees of all shades of green, red, orange, yellow, and brown. Each of these unique trees sprouted from a common ground. Their roots stretched into the same soil. And they were nourished by the same sun and rain.

We human beings are like these trees. We come in many shapes, colors, and sizes. And we express the common spiritual dimension of our humanity in many different ways. Still, we are rooted in the same soil. Although the children in our churches might express their spiritual lives in different ways, each of them (and each of us) needs to be rooted in Christ, the source of our wisdom, the desire of our heart, the giver of our imaginations, and the liberator of our bodies, minds, and souls.

Creating inclusive environments involves helping children whose spiritual lives are centered on words, emotion, symbols, and action to be embraced and affirmed for who they are and how they make meaning and connect with God. But let us remember that the ultimate goal of ministry with children is not to shape children into people whose lives are centered on one (or even all) of the four spiritual styles. Our goal is to trans/form children into disciples of Jesus Christ, young people who are rooted in the transcendent One who came into this earth as a child. And as we seek to build followers of Christ, let's do so in environments of harmonious dissonance, spaces that nurture and challenge young people to have trans/formative encounters with God through words, emotion, symbols, and action. From a common soil, wondrous diversity can grow.

As you consider the ways in which you can create harmoniously dissonant environments, remember the opening words of Dr. Benjamin Spock in his famous book, *The Common Sense Book of Baby and Child Care*: "Trust yourself. You know more than you think you do."[19] And as you trust yourself to create inclusive, nurturing environments, I invite you to open yourself to the wisdom of the children in your midst. Each child brings to the table the gifts of his or her unique perspectives and insights.

May you experience the joy and fulfillment of words, emotion, symbols, and action. And may you share this joy with children.

---

19. Spock, *Common Sense*, 3.

Afterword

YOU'VE JUST WASTED YOUR time reading this book—that is, if you now put it aside without doing anything about it. The subject in which you've immersed yourself for a few hours is a matter of great importance, but relatively few people realize it. Now that you've invested more thought and interest than most people—by actually reading a whole book on the spiritual formation of children—we (the church, the world) need you to join in a growing movement to reinvent and rediscover ministry among children and youth, to help children become authentic followers of God in the way of Jesus, and to do so in ways that honor their different ways of knowing God.

When I was a pastor, a lot of Christians saw kids as "the church of tomorrow," which implied they were not full participants in the church of today. Others saw children as the way to rope in their tithes-paying parents; adults really count, and kids' programs are tasty bait to get them in. Even among the most inventive churches that were rethinking, exploring, and innovating in order to reach youth and young adults, there was little left-over creativity to be sure that today's generation of children wouldn't be taught a lot that they'd have to unlearn in ten or twenty years.

You may remember Dave quoting John Westerhoff in chapter 1 —about children being like saplings: just because they're small doesn't mean they're something less than trees. If we're going to count trees, we need to include the saplings: they count just as much. In fact, if we have much in the way of foresight, maybe for the next few generations we should look at adults as the ones we want to get in the door so that they'll bring their children. Maybe we should start seeing children as the main point, as if the kingdom of God were made up of such as they, crazy as that may sound. Maybe the best energies of our most creative and thoughtful adults should be devoted to a historic refocusing on children.

Maybe I'm overstating the need. But maybe I'm not. Sometimes I think that most adult Christians are so thoroughly entrenched in a constricted version of the faith that we should just let them be, and focus our energies on forming the up-and-coming generation of vibrant Christian disciples. Then I remember that parents play a pretty important role in this process (!), which tends to nudge me closer to a sense of balance. Both children and adults need to benefit from a revolution in Christian education and spiritual formation—a revolution in praxis, defined as practice and theory guiding one another.

This book makes an important contribution to the revolution in children's ministry that needs to happen. Which brings me back to the best ways you can translate your interest into action, now that you've read this book.

First, if you're a parent or a prospective parent, Dave's insights can help you in your vocation of raising your children "in the nurture and love of the Lord" (Eph 6:4). If you're an aunt, uncle, grandparent, or neighbor, these insights can also help you. In hindsight, they will help you see why religious education "took" for some children better than others: for kids who never seemed to "get it," it wasn't necessarily because of the child, but may have been because of a weakness in the one-size-fits-all approach to education. Having finished the book, you might approach that adult son or teenage granddaughter who is disinterested in faith and far from the church these days. You might explain spiritual styles and stir up some meaningful conversation about what worked and didn't work in his or her spiritual formation. You may even discover that there is more spiritual interest under the surface than you previously assumed.

Second, if you're not yet involved in the children's ministry at your church, this is the time to get involved. Or if your church doesn't need you (I'm not sure if that's ever happened!), check out a Christian summer camp or after-school program where you can become a mentor to children "in the ways of the Lord."

Third, if you are already involved (thank God for you!), this is a great time to pull some of the other adult leaders together for a reading group. Start with Dave's book, and make your current case of thinking contagious. Don't be surprised if a lot of your colleagues aren't terribly interested; just be grateful they're serving. But find one or two—that's a great start—and strike a little spark of creative thinking together. Remember that old campfire song about it only taking a spark?

Fourth, if you have the gifts to do so, start experimenting. Use the spiritual styles Dave has introduced you to as a stimulus to creative teaching. We need curricula and learning resources to be designed and written with these different styles in mind. We need to get beyond the old industrial-processes model, as if kids could be spiritually formed through an assembly-line, one-size-fits-all process.

Fifth, become an advocate in your church and denomination for a gentle revolution in children's ministry. Budgets are moral documents, and they reflect priorities—so investing in your children's ministry should actually show up as a significant slice in your pie charts. Do you have professional staff in children's ministry? If not, might this be a goal to champion? If so, what investments in courses, conferences, and mentoring would help your staff become more motivated and equipped? How about volunteers—what investments are you making in their education and development? What results might you expect from a well-planned day of appreciation, fun, and high-quality training for your volunteers? Wouldn't an investment like this show how important they are to your church—and how important the children they serve are?

Beyond increasing our commitment to special programs for children, we need to find ways to have kids not simply be one slice of the pie, but rather be a high-priority concern integrated into every part of the pie of congregational life. What would happen if in all our congregational planning we sought to honor children, facilitate their participation, and engage their varying spiritual styles?

And finally, if you haven't done so already, realize that you once were a child, and from God's perspective, you are still one now. Realize that you have a spiritual style, and start investing in your own spiritual formation with greater sensitivity to your style, being careful not to close yourself to other styles. Loving others as yourself requires that you take care of yourself . . . and Dave's book can start helping you help you, which will then overflow to others.

There is already sufficient data to tell us that we're having a terrible retention crisis in the Christian faith. Instead of saying, "What's wrong with young people today?" we need to realize that the version of Christian faith they are learning from their parents and their churches simply isn't compelling enough to earn their lasting commitment. The rising church drop-out rates from one generation to the next aren't simply a problem to be solved; they are a reality that is trying to teach us something. In finding what the children need, we will, I believe, have the opportunity to rediscover what our faith is all about. We will rediscover that our faith was never intended to be a one-size-fits-all affair designed for compliant grown-ups who know how to fit in with the program. Rather, it was from the start a creative, multi-faceted community that engaged a variety of people—including the very young—in a variety of ways.

That sense of creativity and variety—in age and in spiritual styles— is something we seemed to lose in the modern era, with its emphasis on homogeneity and standardization. Thank God for books like this one—that help us realize what we lost in the past and what we lack in the present so we can regain it for a more robust future. Thank God for readers like you—who will join with the author and thousands of other readers in realizing that future.

Could there be a more supremely worthwhile investment of time, intelligence, money, and energy, for our children's sake, for our own, for future generations yet unborn, and for the sake of Jesus and the kingdom of God?

Brian D. McLaren
author (brianmclaren.net)

Practices for Nurturing Children's Spirituality

WORD-CENTERED CHILDREN

Younger Children (approximately 6 years old and younger):

- Read age-appropriate Bibles and books (cloth books, board books, picture books, coloring books)
- Encourage children to learn and memorize short Bible verses using games and actions
- Teach rhymes that include Bible references, Christian values, prayers, and spiritual topics
- Set up a story corner for children to use at their own leisure and have a story time during each program or devotion

Middle Children (approximately 6–11 years old):

- Take a close look at the lyrics of hymns/songs that your children know—study the lyrics together and connect them to Scripture or lessons
- Include Bible study as part of family devotions and church programs
- Go to a bookstore (religious or otherwise) and let your children select a book of their choice
- Give children access to Bible fact books

Older Children (approximately 11–14 years old):

- Play Bible quizzing games, being careful not to encourage too much competition

- Provide resources for personal Bible study (dictionaries, encyclopedias, Bible study guides, etc.)

- Teach children about Bible translating by studying the same passage from several different translations

- Study maps with children to teach about the Bible, church history, and contemporary issues—maps can include ancient Israel, Paul's travels, religion across Europe during the Reformation, and the Reverse Map (in which the Southern Hemisphere is at the top)

- Give young people notebooks and encourage them to write a reflective journal

EMOTION-CENTERED CHILDREN

Younger Children (approximately 6 years old and younger):

- Provide simple percussion instruments for children to play during times of music

- Encourage children to dance freely and playfully and creatively

- Have children draw pictures that depict how they are feeling

- Use appropriate physical contact with children so they know they are loved

Middle Children (approximately 6–11 years old):

- Create spaces that are safe for children to talk about their feelings—share your feelings in appropriate ways with the children as well

- Have CD players and headphones with music for children to listen to on their own

- Start a children's choir or dance troupe

- Have banners or flags for children to use when dancing or listening to music

- Host a music camp or drama program for children in your church and neighborhood

Older Children (approximately 11–14 years old):

- Watch Christian music videos and recordings of concerts with children

- Help the children put on a play—make costumes, sets, and props and perform it for the congregation

- Allow young people the freedom to respond to music as they see fit (clapping, raising hands, swaying, etc.)

- Write songs with children based on a Bible passage, a lesson, or a particular theme

SYMBOL-CENTERED CHILDREN

Younger Children (approximately 6 years old and younger):

- Go to a local pond or park and feed the ducks or squirrels

- Provide children with many different types of supplies for creating artwork

- Bake bread together, bless it, and eat it together

- Go on a nature walk with children, allowing them some freedom to run, skip, and play among God's creation

Middle Children (approximately 6–11 years old):

- Help children plant a garden—flowers, vegetables, or both

- Make a prayer corner or nook

- Include many kinds of prayers in ministries and family devotions

- Provide a time during which children can reflect on images and icons (Stations of the Cross, stained glass windows, artwork, etc.)

- Begin a program or devotion by lighting a candle to symbolize Christ's presence

Older Children (approximately 11–14 years old):

- Create a ritual meal for a special occasion (Christmas, Easter, All Saints Day), having children select foods that are symbolic of the occasion
- Create a labyrinth and teach young people how to meditate as they walk along this symbolic pilgrimage
- Have children light candles to represent lifting their concerns to God
- Include a moment of silence in your ministries or family time

ACTION-CENTERED CHILDREN

Younger Children (approximately 6 years old and younger):

- Help children put together care packages for needy children
- Sponsor a child as a family or Sunday school class—and don't forget to write to your sponsor child often
- Volunteer with children at a soup kitchen or food bank
- Decorate a Christmas tree with paper ornaments that have the gender and age of a needy child—families can take an ornament, buy a gift for this child, and put it under the tree with the tag attached to it

Middle Children (approximately 6–11 years old):

- Take children to visit people in a hospital or retirement home
- Raise money for a certain cause through carol singing, garage sales, car washes, or bake sales—and don't forget to track your progress
- Take notice and talk about how accessible your church/home/school would be for people with disabilities
- Cook a meal or bake cookies together and take it to a family in need or in crisis
- Help children run a social justice awareness board for your congregation—choose one issue each month (hunger, environmental degradation, child labor, racism, etc.)

Older Children (approximately 11–14 years old):

- Send or sponsor young people on a summer exchange program or encourage them to volunteer at a camp for disadvantaged children

- Help children trick-or-treat for canned foods to be donated to a local food bank instead of collecting candy

- Organize a fair-trade expo or sale

- Focus on one issue—do research, petition, and raise awareness about one specific justice issue

Bibliography

Allen, Holly Catterton. "Exploring Children's Spirituality from a Christian Perspective." In *Nurturing Children's Spirituality: Christian Perspectives and Best Practices*, edited by Holly Catterton Allen, 5–20. Eugene, OR: Cascade, 2008.

———. "Nurturing Children's Spirituality in Intergenerational Christian Settings." In *Children's Spirituality: Christian Perspectives, Research, and Applications*, edited by Donald Ratcliff, 266–83. Eugene, OR: Cascade, 2004.

———. "Theological Perspectives on Children in the Church: Anabaptist/Believers Churches. In *Nurturing Children's Spirituality: Christian Perspectives and Best Practices*, edited by Holly Catterton Allen, 110–26. Eugene, OR: Cascade, 2008.

Anthony, Michael J. "Putting Children's Spirituality in Perspective. In *Perspectives on Children's Spiritual Formation: Four Views*, edited by Michael J. Anthony, 1–43. Nashville: Broadman & Holman, 2006.

Ariès, Philippe. *Centuries of Childhood: A Social History of Family Life*. Translated by Robert Baldick. New York: Vintage, 1962.

Arnett, Jeffrey Jensen. "Suffering, Selfish, Slackers? Myths and Reality About Emerging Adults." *Journal of Youth and Adolescence* 36 (2007) 23–29.

Baker, Dori Grinenko, and Joyce Ann Mercer. *Lives to Offer: Accompanying Youth on Their Vocational Quests*. Cleveland: Pilgrim, 2007.

Barna, George. *Transforming Children into Spiritual Champions: Why Children Should Be Your Church's #1 Priority.* Ventura, CA: Regal, 2003.

Bartholomew, Craig G., and Michael W. Goheen. *The Drama of Scripture: Finding Our Place in the Biblical Story*. Grand Rapids: Baker Academic, 2004.

Beckwith, Ivy. *Formational Children's Ministry: Shaping Children Using Story, Ritual, and Relationship*. Grand Rapids: Baker, 2010.

Bell, Rob. *Everything is Spiritual*. DVD. Grand Rapids: Zondervan, 2007.

———. *Velvet Elvis: Repainting the Christian Faith*. Grand Rapids: Zondervan, 2005.

Bellous, Joyce E. "Editorial." *International Journal of Children's Spirituality* 13:3 (2008) 195–201.

———. *Educating Faith: An Approach to Christian Formation*. Toronto: Clements, 2006.

———. "Five Classroom Activities for Sustaining a Spiritual Environment." *International Journal of Children's Spirituality* 11:1 (2006) 99–111.

Bellous, Joyce E., and David M. Csinos. "Spiritual Styles: Creating an Environment to Nurture Spiritual Wholeness." *International Journal of Children's Spirituality* 14:3 (2009) 213–24.

Bellous, Joyce E., et al. *Spiritual Styles: Assessing What Really Matters*. Edmonton: Tall Pine, 2009.

———. *Spiritual Styles—Children's Version: Assessing What Really Matters*. Edmonton: Tall Pine, 2009.

Bellous, Joyce E., and Dan Sheffield. *Conversations that Change Us: Learning the Arts of Theological Reflection*. Toronto: Clements, 2007.

Benson, Peter L., et al. "Spiritual Development in Childhood and Adolescence: Toward a Field of Inquiry." *Applied Developmental Science* 7:3 (2003) 205–13.

Berryman, Jerome W. *Godly Play: An Imaginative Approach to Religious Education*. Minneapolis: Augsburg, 2001.

———. *Teaching Godly Play: How to Mentor the Spiritual Development of Children*. Denver: Morehouse, 2009.

Bibby, Reginald W., et al. *The Emerging Millennials: How Canada's Newest Generation is Responding to Change and Choice*. Lethbridge, AB: Project Canada, 2009.

Boso, Marianna, et al. "Neurophysiology and Neurobiology of the Musical Experience." *Functional Neurology* 21:3 (2006) 187–91.

Boyatzis, Chris. "Children's Spiritual Development: Advancing the Field in Definition, Measurement, and Theory." In *Nurturing Children's Spirituality: Christian Perspectives and Best Practices*, edited by Holly Catterton Allen, 43–57. Eugene, OR: Cascade, 2008.

Boyatzis, Chris J., and Babette T. Newman. "How Shall We Study Children's Spirituality?" In *Children's Spirituality: Christian Perspectives, Research, and Applications*, edited by Donald Ratcliff, 166–81. Eugene, OR: Cascade, 2004.

Brueggemann, Walter. *Belonging and Growing in the Christian Community: The First Years of Parenting*. Atlanta: General Assembly Mission Board, Presbyterian Church in the United States, 1979.

———. *The Creative Word: Canon as a Model for Biblical Education*. Philadelphia: Fortress, 1982.

Bushnell, Horace. *Christian Nurture*. New York: Charles Scribner's Sons, 1876.

Carlson, Gregory C., and John K. Crupper. "Instructional-Analytic Model." In *Perspectives on Children's Spiritual Formation: Four Views*, edited by Michael J. Anthony, 103–63. Nashville: Broadman & Holman, 2006.

Cascante-Gómez, Fernando A. "Countercultural Autobiography: Stories from the Underside and Education for Justice." *Religious Education* 102:3 (2007) 279–87.

Cashdan, Sheldon. *Object Relations Therapy: Using the Relationship*. New York: Norton, 1988.

Cavalletti, Sofia. *The Religious Potential of the Child: Experiencing Scripture and Liturgy with Young Children*. Translated by Patricia M. Coulter and Julie M. Coulter. New York: Paulist, 1993.

Chapman, Kathleen. *Teaching Kids Authentic Worship: How to Keep Them Close to God for Life*. Grand Rapids: Baker, 2003.

Clark, Alison. "The Mosaic Approach and Research with Young Children." In *The Reality of Research with Children and Young People*, edited by Vicky Lewis et al., 142–56. London: Sage, 2004.

Coles, Robert. *The Spiritual Life of Children*. Boston: Houghton Mifflin, 1990.

Cone, James H. *Black Theology and Black Power*. Maryknoll: Orbis, 1997.

Crain, Margaret Ann. "Reconsidering the Power of Story in Religious Education." *Religious Education* 102:3 (2007) 241–48.

Crozier, Karen and Elizabeth Conde-Frazier. "A Narrative of Children's Spirituality: African American and Latino Theological Perspectives." In *Children's Spirituality: Christian Perspectives, Research, and Applications*, edited by Donald Ratcliff, 284–308. Eugene, OR: Cascade, 2004.

Csinos, David M. "The Biblical Theme of Welcoming Children." *McMaster Journal of Theology and Ministry* 8 (2007) 97–117.

———. "'Come, Follow Me': Apprenticeship in Jesus' Approach to Education." *Religious Education* 105:1 (2010) 45–62.

Csinos, David M., et al. "Where are the Children? Keeping Sight of Young Disciples in the Emerging Church Movement." *Journal of Family and Community Ministries: Empowering through Faith* 23:4 (2010) 10–21.

Dawn, Marva J. *Is It a Lost Cause? Having the Heart of God for the Church's Children.* Grand Rapids: Eerdmans, 1997.

de Souza, Marian. "Educating for Hope, Compassion, and Meaning in a Diverse and Intolerant World." *International Journal of Children's Spirituality* 11:1 (2006) 165–75.

Douglas, Mary. *Natural Symbols: Explorations in Cosmology.* 2nd ed. London: Routledge, 1996.

Dykstra, Craig. *Growing in the Life of Faith: Education and Christian Practices.* Louisville: Geneva, 1999.

Eisner, Elliot W. *The Educational Imagination: On the Design and Evaluation of School Programs.* 2nd ed. New York: Macmillan, 1985.

Elkind, David. *A Sympathetic Understanding of the Child: Birth to Sixteen.* 3rd ed. Boston: Allyn and Bacon, 1994.

Emond, Ruth. "Ethnographic Research Methods with Children and Young People." In *Researching Children's Experience: Approaches and Methods,* edited by Sheila Greene and Diane Hogan, 123–39. London: Sage, 2005.

Erickson, David V. "Spirituality, Loss, and Recovery in Children with Disabilities." *International Journal of Children's Spirituality* 13:3 (2008) 287–96.

Erricker, Clive. "Against the Protection of Childhood Innocence." *International Journal of Children's Spirituality* 8:1 (2003) 3–7.

Ford, Victoria M. and Esther Wong. "Narrative and the Moral Education of the Christian Child." In *Children's Spirituality: Christian Perspectives, Research, and Applications,* edited by Donald Ratcliff, 309–23. Eugene, OR: Cascade, 2004.

Foster, Richard J. *Celebration of Discipline: The Path to Spiritual Growth.* San Francisco: HarperSanFrancisco, 1978.

Fowler, Larry. *Rock-Solid Kids: Giving Children a Biblical Foundation for Life.* Ventura, CA: Gospel Light, 2004.

Free the Children. "2010 We Day: About the Day." No pages. Online: http://weday.free thechildren.com/about.

———. "FTC Curriculum." No pages. Online: http://www.freethechildren.com/get involved/educator/programs.php?type=curriculum.

Freire, Paulo. *Pedagogy of the Oppressed,* 30th Anniversary Edition. Translated by Myra Bergman Ramos. New York: Continuum, 2007.

Garbarino, James, et al. *What Children Can Tell Us: Eliciting, Interpreting, and Evaluating Critical Information from Children.* San Francisco: Jossey-Bass, 1992.

Gerbner, George. "Reclaiming Our Cultural Mythology." *In Context* 38 (1994). No pages. Online: http://www.context.org/ICLIB/IC38/Gerbner.htm.

Graves, Trisha. "Pragmatic-Participatory Model." In *Perspectives on Children's Spiritual Formation: Four Views,* edited by Michael J. Anthony, 165–223. Nashville: Broadman & Holman, 2006.

Greig, Anne, et al. *Doing Research with Children.* 2nd ed. London: Sage, 2007.

Grenz, Stanley J., et al. *Pocket Dictionary of Theological Terms*. Downer's Grove, IL: InterVarsity, 1999.

Graham, Billy. "Billy Graham: Bible is God's 'Love Letter' to Us." *Seattle Post-Intelligencer*, September 6, 2007. http://www.seattlepi.com/graham/327551_billy907.html.

Groome, Thomas H. *Christian Religious Education: Sharing Our Story and Vision*. San Francisco: HarperSanFrancisco, 1980.

————. *Sharing Faith: A Comprehensive Approach to Religious Education and Pastoral Ministry*. San Francisco: HarperSanFrancisco, 1991.

Hamilton, N. Gregory. *Self and Others: Object Relations Theory in Practice*. Northvale, NJ: Jason Aronson, 1990.

Hardy, Alister. *The Living Stream: A Restatement of Evolution Theory and its Relation to the Spirit of Man*. London: Collins, 1965.

Hart, Tobin. "Spiritual Experiences and Capacities of Children and Youth." In *The Handbook of Spiritual Development in Childhood and Adolescence*, edited by Eugene C. Roehlkepartain et al., 163–77. Thousand Oaks, CA: Sage, 2006.

Hawkins, Greg. "Watch Greg Hawkins: Hear the Heart Behind *Reveal*." No pages. Online: http://revealnow.com/story.asp?storyid=48.

Hawkins, Greg and Cally Parkinson. *Reveal: Where are You?* Barrington, IL: Willow Creek Association, 2007.

Hay, David. "The Naturalness of Relational Consciousness." In *The Spirit of the Child*. Rev. ed., David Hay and Rebecca Nye, 131–45. London: Jessica Kingsley, 2006.

Hay, David and Rebecca Nye. *The Spirit of the Child*. Rev. ed. London: Jessica Kingsley, 2006.

Heller, David. *The Children's God*. Chicago: University of Chicago Press, 1986.

Herzog, Kristin. *Children and Our Global Future: Theological and Social Challenges*. Cleveland: Pilgrim, 2005.

Hill, Malcolm. "Ethical Considerations in Researching Children's Experiences." In *Researching Children's Experience: Approaches and Methods*, edited by Sheila Greene and Diane Hogan, 61–86. London: Sage, 2005.

Holmes, Robyn M. *Fieldwork with Children*. Thousand Oaks, CA: Sage, 1998.

Holmes, Urban T. *A History of Christian Spirituality: An Analytical Introduction*. New York: Seabury, 1980.

Hood, Dana Kennamer. "Six Children Seeking God: Exploring Childhood Spiritual Development in Context." In *Children's Spirituality: Christian Perspectives, Research, and Applications*, edited by Donald Ratcliff, 233–48. Eugene, OR: Cascade, 2004.

Hopkins, Mary Rice. "How to Lead Music with Kids." In *Children's Ministry that Works: The Basics and Beyond*. Rev. ed., 114–20. Loveland, CO: Group, 2002.

Hoyt, Thomas Jr. "Testimony." In *Practicing Our Faith: A Way of Life for a Searching People*, edited by Dorothy C. Bass, 91–103. San Francisco: Jossey-Bass, 1997.

Ireland, Alexander. *The Book-Lover's Enchiridion: A Treasury of Thoughts on the Solace and Companionship of Books*. London: Simpkin, Marshall, and Co., 1888.

Jackson, Michael. Interview by Oprah Winfrey, February 10, 1993.

Jensen, David H. *Graced Vulnerability: A Theology of Childhood*. Cleveland: Pilgrim, 2005.

Jones, Tony. *The Sacred Way: Spiritual Practices of Everyday Life*. Grand Rapids: Zondervan/Youth Specialties, 2005.

————. *Soul Shaper: Exploring Spirituality and Contemplative Practices in Youth Ministry*. Grand Rapids: Zondervan/Youth Specialties, 2003.

Jung, C. G. *Modern Man in Search of a Soul.* Translated by W. S. Dell and Cary F. Bagnes. San Diego: Harcourt, 1933.

Kegan, Robert. *The Evolving Self: Problem and Process in Human Development.* Cambridge, MA: Harvard University Press, 1982.

Kelcourse, Felicity B., ed. *Human Development and Faith: Life-Cycle Stages of Body, Mind, and Soul.* St. Louis: Chalice, 2004.

Kielburger, Craig. "Free the Children: The World's Largest Network of Children Helping Children through Education." In *Notes from Canada's Young Activists: A Generation Stands Up for Change,* edited by Severn Cullis-Suzuki et al., 96–105. Vancouver: Greystone, 2007.

Kielburger, Craig, and Marc Kielburger. *Me to We: Finding Meaning in a Material World.* New York: Fireside, 2004.

Kielburger, Marc, and Craig Kielburger. *Take Action! A Guide to Active Citizenship.* Hoboken, NJ: John Wiley & Sons, 2002.

King, Martin Luther, Jr. "Letter from Birmingham City Jail (1963)." In *A Testament of Hope: The Essential Writings and Speeches of Martin Luther King, Jr.,* edited by James Melvin Washington, 289–302. New York: HarperCollins, 1986.

Klein, Josephine. *Our Need for Others and its Roots in Infancy.* London: Tavistock, 1987.

Klein, Randall S. *Object Relations and the Family Process.* New York: Praeger, 1990.

Klepsch, Marvin, and Laura Logie. *Children Draw and Tell: An Introduction to the Projective Uses of Children's Human Figure Drawings.* New York: Brunner/Mazel, 1982.

Lave, Jean, and Etienne Wenger. *Situated Learning: Legitimate Peripheral Participation.* Cambridge: Cambridge University Press, 1991.

Lloyd-Smith, Mel, and Jane Tarr. "Researching Children's Perspectives: A Sociological Dimension." In *Researching Children's Perspectives,* edited by Ann Lewis and Geoff Lindsay, 59–70. Buckingham, PA: Open University Press, 2000.

Locke, John. *An Essay Concerning Human Understanding,* edited by Peter H. Nidditch. Oxford: Oxford University Press, 1975.

Louv, Richard. *Last Child in the Woods: Saving Our Children from Nature-Deficit Disorder.* Chapel Hill: Algonquin, 2005.

Lusk, Rich. *Paedofaith: A Primer on the Mystery of Infant Salvation and a Handbook for Covenant Parents.* Monroe, LA: Athanasius, 2005.

Lykes, M. Brinton. "Creative Arts and Photography in Participatory Action Research in Guatemala." In *Handbook of Action Research,* edited by Peter Reason and Hilary Bradbury, 363–71. London: Sage, 2001.

Magill, Lucanne. "Music Therapy in Spirituality." *Music Therapy Today* (2002) 1–7. Online: http://mttd.com/modules/mmmagazine/issues/20021205144406/200212 05145915/Magill.pdf.

Mampe, Birgit, et al. "Newborns' Cry Melody is Shaped by their Native Language." *Current Biology* 19:23 (2009) 1994–97.

Mandell, Nancy. "The Least-Adult Role in Studying Children." *Journal of Contemporary Ethnography* 16:4 (1988) 433–67.

May, Scottie. "The Contemplative-Reflective Model." In *Perspectives on Children's Spiritual Formation: Four Views,* edited by Michael J. Anthony, 45–102. Nashville: Broadman & Holman, 2006.

May, Scottie, et al. *Children Matter: Celebrating Their Place in the Church, Family, and Community.* Grand Rapids: Eerdmans, 2005.

May, Scottie and Donald Ratcliff. "Children's Spiritual Experiences and the Brain." In *Children's Spirituality: Christian Perspectives, Research, and Applications*, edited by Donald Ratcliff, 149–65. Eugene, OR: Cascade, 2004.

McLaren, Brian D. *Everything Must Change: Jesus, Global Crises, and a Revolution of Hope*. Nashville: Thomas Nelson, 2007.

———. *Finding Our Way Again: The Return of the Ancient Practices*. Nashville: Thomas Nelson, 2008.

———. *A New Kind of Christianity: Ten Questions that are Transforming the Faith*. New York: HarperOne, 2010.

———. *The Story We Find Ourselves In: Further Adventures of a New Kind of Christian*. San Francisco: Jossey-Bass, 2003.

Mecum, Shelly. *God's Photo Album*. San Francisco: Harper, 2001.

Mercer, Joyce Ann. *Welcoming Children: A Practical Theology of Childhood*. St. Louis: Chalice, 2005.

Miller, Sue, and David Staal. *Making Your Children's Ministry the Best Hour of Every Kid's Week*. Grand Rapids: Zondervan, 2004.

Miller-McLemore, Bonnie J. *In the Midst of Chaos: Caring for Children as Spiritual Practice*. San Francisco: Jossey-Bass, 2007.

Mintz, Steven. *Huck's Raft: A History of American Childhood*. Cambridge, MA: Belknap/ Harvard University Press, 2004.

Myers, Barbara Kimes. *Young Children and Spirituality*. New York: Routledge, 1997.

Nesbitt, Eleanor. "Researching 8 to 13-Year-Olds' Perspectives on Their Experience of Religion." In *Researching Children's Perspectives*, edited by Ann Lewis and Geoff Lindsay, 135–49. Buckingham, PA: Open University Press, 2000.

Ng, David, and Virginia Thomas. *Children in the Worshipping Community*. Atlanta: John Knox, 1981.

Nye, Rebecca. "Christian Perspectives on Children's Spirituality: Social Science Contributions?" In *Children's Spirituality: Christian Perspectives, Research, and Applications*, edited by Donald Ratcliff, 90–107. Eugene, OR: Cascade, 2004.

———. "Identifying the Core of Children's Spirituality." In *The Spirit of the Child*. Rev. ed., David Hay and Rebecca Nye, 108–28. London: Jessica Kingsley, 2006.

———. "Relational Consciousness and the Spiritual Lives of Children: Convergence with Children's Theory of Mind?" In *Psychological Studies of Spiritual and Religious Development: Being Human: The Case for Religion*, vol. 2, edited by K. Helmut Reich et al., 57–82. Lengerich, Germany: Pabst, 1999.

O'Brien, Roger. "4 Ways to Become Holy." *U.S. Catholic* 61:3 (1996) 17–23.

Persinger, Michael A. "The Temporal Lobe: The Biological Basis of the God Experience." In *NeuroTheology: Brain, Science, Spirituality, Religious Experience*, edited by R. Joseph, 273–78. San Jose: University Press, 2003.

Petőfi, Sándor. "Nemzeti Dal." In *The Spirit of Hungary*, by Stephen Sisa, 149. Toronto: Rákóczi, 1983.

Pritchard, Gretchen Wolff. *Offering the Gospel to Children*. Cambridge, MA: Cowley, 1992.

Ratcliff, Donald. "The Beginnings of a Christian Perspective on Qualitative Research." Online: http://qualitativeresearch.ratcliffs.net/christianperspective.pdf.

———. "Music, God, and Psychology." *Journal of the American Scientific Affiliation* 35:2 (1983). No pages. Online: http://www.asa3.org/ASA/PSCF/1983/JASA6-83Ratcliff.html.

————. "Qualitative Research Methods." No pages. Online: http://qualitativeresearch .ratcliffs.net.

————. "Rituals in a School Hallway: Evidence of a Latent Spirituality of Children." *Christian Education Journal* 5 (2001) 9–26.

Ratcliff, Donald, and Scottie May. "Identifying Children's Spirituality, Walter Wangerin's Perspectives, and an Overview of this Book." In *Children's Spirituality: Christian Perspectives, Research, and Applications*, edited by Donald Ratcliff, 7–21. Eugene, OR: Cascade, 2004.

Ratcliff, Donald, and Rebecca Nye. "Childhood Spirituality: Strengthening the Research Foundation." In *The Handbook of Spiritual Development in Childhood and Adolescence*, edited by Eugene C. Roehlkepartain et al., 473–83. Thousand Oaks, CA: Sage, 2006.

Richards, Lawrence O. *A Theology of Children's Ministry*. Grand Rapids: Zondervan, 1983.

Rizzuto, Ana-Maria. *The Birth of the Living God: A Psychoanalytic Study*. Chicago: University of Chicago Press, 1979.

Roberts, Helen. "Listening to Children: and Hearing Them." In *Research with Children: Perspectives and Practices*, 2nd ed., edited by Pia Christensen and Allison James, 260–75. London: Falmer, 2008.

Roehlkepartain, Eugene C. "Exploring Scientific and Theological Perspectives on Children's Spirituality." In *Children's Spirituality: Christian Perspectives, Research, and Applications*, edited by Donald Ratcliff, 120–32. Eugene, OR: Cascade, 2004.

Roehlkepartain, Eugene C., and Eboo Patel. "Congregations: Unexamined Crucibles for Spiritual Development." In *The Handbook of Spiritual Development in Childhood and Adolescence*, edited by Eugene C. Roehlkepartain et al., 324–36. Thousand Oaks, CA: Sage, 2006.

Rollins, Peter. *How (not) to Speak of God*. Brewster, MA: Paraclete, 2006.

————. *The Fidelity of Betrayal: Towards a Church Beyond Belief*. Brewster, MA: Paraclete, 2008.

Rubin, Jeffrey. "Psychoanalytic Treatment with a Buddhist Mediator." In *Object Relations Theory and Religion: Clinical Applications*, edited by Mark Finn and John Gartner, 87–107. Westport, CT: Praeger, 1992.

Russell, Letty M. *Just Hospitality: God's Welcome in a World of Difference*. Edited by J. Shannon Clarkson and Kate M. Ott. Louisville: Westminster John Knox, 2009.

Saliers, Don E. "Singing Our Lives." In *Practicing Our Faith: A Way of Life for a Searching People*, edited by Dorothy C. Bass, 179–93. San Francisco: Jossey-Bass, 1997.

Samaritan's Purse. "Uplifting the Outcasts." No pages. Online: http://www.samaritanspurse .org/index.php/articles/uplifting_the_outcasts/.

Seymour, Jack L. "Editorial: Tell Me a Story." *Religious Education* 102:3 (2007) 237–39.

Sheldrake, Philip. "What is Spirituality?" In *Exploring Christian Spirituality: An Ecumenical Reader*, edited by Kenneth J. Collins, 21–42. Grand Rapids: Baker, 2000.

Sisemore, Timothy. "Theological Perspectives on Children in the Church: Reformed and Presbyterian." In *Nurturing Children's Spirituality: Christian Perspectives and Best Practices*, edited by Holly Catterton Allen, 93–109. Eugene, OR: Cascade, 2008.

Smith, Christian with Melinda Lundquist Denton. *Soul Searching: The Religious and Spiritual Lives of American Teenagers*. Oxford: Oxford University Press, 2005.

Smith, Christian with Patricia Snell. *Souls in Transition: The Religious and Spiritual Lives of Emerging Adults*. Oxford: Oxford University Press, 2009.

Smith, Tim. *The Danger of Raising Nice Kids: Preparing Our Children to Change Their World*. Downer's Grove, IL: InterVarsity, 2006.

Spock, Benjamin. *The Common Sense Book of Baby and Child Care*. New York: Duell, Sloan, and Pearce, 1946.

St. Clair, Michael. *Human Relationships and the Experience of God: Object Relations and Religion*. Eugene, OR: Wipf & Stock, 1994.

———. *Object Relations and Self Psychology: An Introduction*. 2nd ed. Pacific Grove, CA: Brooks/Cole, 1996.

Stewart, Sonja M., and Jerome W. Berryman. *Young Children and Worship*. Louisville: Westminster John Knox, 1989.

Stonehouse, Catherine. *Joining Children on the Spiritual Journey: Nurturing a Life of Faith*. Grand Rapids: Baker, 1998.

———. "Knowing God in Childhood: A Study of Godly Play and the Spirituality of Children." *Christian Education Journal* 5 (2001) 27–45.

Stonehouse, Catherine and Scottie May. *Listening to Children on the Spiritual Journey: Guidance for Those Who Teach and Nurture*. Grand Rapids: Baker Academic, 2010.

Sutherland, Neil. *Children in English-Canadian Society: Framing the Twentieth-Century Consensus*. Toronto: University of Toronto Press, 1976.

Thomas à Kempis. *The Imitation of Christ*. Translated by Richard Whitford. New York: Pocket, 1954.

Tye, Karen B. *Basics of Christian Education*. St. Louis: Chalice, 2000.

Veale, Angela. "Creative Methodologies in Participatory Research with Children." In *Researching Children's Experience: Approaches and Methods*, edited by Sheila Greene and Diane Hogan, 253–72. London: Sage, 2005.

Vygotsky, L. S. *Mind in Society: The Development of Higher Psychological Processes*. Cambridge, MA: Harvard University Press, 1978.

Wallis, Jim. *The Great Awakening: Reviving Faith & Politics in a Post-Religious Right America*. New York: HarperOne, 2008.

Ware, Corinne. *Discover Your Spiritual Type: A Guide to Individual and Congregational Growth*. Bethesda, MD: Alban Institute, 2000.

Wenger, Etienne. *Communities of Practice: Learning, Meaning, and Identity*. Cambridge: Cambridge University Press, 1998.

Westerhoff, John H. III. "The Church's Contemporary Challenge: Assisting Adults to Mature Spiritually *with* Their Children." In *Nurturing Children's Spirituality: Christian Perspectives and Best Practices*, edited by Holly Catterton Allen, 355–65. Eugene, OR: Cascade, 2008.

———. *Will Our Children Have Faith?* Rev. ed. Harrisburg, PA: Morehouse, 2000.

White, Michael, and David Epston. *Narrative Means to Therapeutic Ends*. New York: Norton, 1990.

Willard, Dallas. *The Divine Conspiracy: Rediscovering Our Hidden Life in God*. San Francisco: HarperSanFrancisco, 1997.

———. *The Spirit of the Disciplines: Understanding How God Changes Lives*. San Francisco: HarperSanFrancisco, 1988.

Willow Creek Association. "The REVEAL Story." No Pages. Online: http://revealnow .com/ storyPage.asp?pageid=26.

Wimberly, Anne E. Streaty. *Soul Stories: African American Christian Education*. Rev. ed. Nashville: Abingdon, 2005.

Wlodarczyk, Natalie. "The Effect of Music Therapy on the Spirituality of Persons in an In-Patient Hospice Unit as Measured by Self-Report." *Journal of Music Therapy* 44:2 (2007) 113–22.

Yoder, John Howard. *Anabaptism and Reformation in Switzerland: An Historical and Theological Analysis of the Dialogues between Anabaptists and Reformers.* Kitchener, ON: Pandora, 2004.

Yust, Karen Marie. "Creating a Spiritual World for Children to Inhabit." *Family Ministry* 18:4 (2004) 24–39.

———. *Real Kids, Real Faith: Practices for Nurturing Children's Spiritual Lives.* San Francisco: Jossey-Bass, 2004.

Printed in Great Britain
by Amazon.co.uk, Ltd.,
Marston Gate.